When the unthinkable happens...

Be Prepared!
Be Ready!

A guide on the impact of crisis events on real estate, insurance, and other businesses, along with the significance of **resiliency**, **sustainability**, and **safety**. Learn how disasters and crises teach us humanity, and give us time to pause and change the course of our lives and finances.

#1 in New Releases
Survival & Preparedness and Real Estate

Coni K. Meyers, LMC, CBLC, CDC

Founder & CEO of CKM Solutions Group

Founder & CEO CKM Preparedness Foundation

Sir. J. Glen Wagstaff, Esq

Founder & CEO of IMPowerED Enterprises, Inc

Board Member of CKM Preparedness Foundation

CKM PREPAREDNESS FOUNDATION

(CKMP is a 501c3)

This book is a tool that provides important information and is a valuable reference guide for individuals and businesses when preparing, surviving, and recovering from disasters and other crises. It also discusses what to do to be sustainable. Review this book each year to update kits, plans, and risk factors. Determine what additional mitigation or sustainability measures can be taken physically and financially to make your family and business more secure.

Our mission: "To provide educational services and programs to help individuals, businesses, and communities become more sustainable, prepared, and ready for disasters and other crises."

Initiatives to be provided:

Kits4Kids
Kits4Pets
Kits4Seniors
Kits4Disabled
Customized Programs for Communities

****QR Code at the end of the book include BONUS items for planning and implementation!****

What Others Are Saying About This Book:

"There could not be a better time for this book. I believe helping others is the best way for people to grow and lead. *When the Unthinkable Happens* will help you with both. I believe in it so strongly we have partnered with Coni to help our brokers and agents be prepared practically, physically, and mentally for any type of disaster along with the communities they serve. Coni has a goal to help millions, and I believe she will. I hope you are one of them."

Tami Bonnell
CEO EXIT Realty Corp International

"Coni Meyers has drawn upon her extensive experience as a FEMA instructor and trainer to write an excellent guide to help consumers and businesses be ready for and recover from a variety of natural and man-man disasters. Her advice, insights, and recommendations are right on target, which makes *When the Unthinkable Happens* the right book, at the right time, for all the right reasons. Since you never know when the next disaster will strike, everyone should keep this book within easy reach."

Edward Segal
Author, *Crisis Ahead: 101 Ways to Prepare For And Bounce Back From Disasters, Scandals, And Other Emergencies*

"Coni Meyer's new book, *When the Unthinkable Happens,* should be read by all of us. You never know when you will encounter an emergency. The time to prepare is before the disaster occurs. Coni covers many pertinent and important subjects like fear and procrastination, taking an inventory of how prepared you are and how to make plans today so you can be prepared when disaster comes to you. The time to prepare for a disaster is now. Get this book, make your plan, and use your plan when disaster strikes!"

Frank DiBartolomeo, DTM, BSEE, MSEE, MIT, CSEP
Lieutenant Colonel, USAF (Ret) and President, DiBartolomeo Consulting International (DCI), LLC

"Written by a retired FEMA inspector, this book takes the reader through man-made and natural disasters and the steps that need to be taken in order to prepare for, survive, and recover from these events. Statistics are cited to remind us that these events do happen and that being prepared is the best way to have the confidence and skill to weather them. A must-read for anyone interested in keeping themselves and their loved ones safe."

Sharron Richardson
Vice President, Broker Services EXIT Realty Corp International

"In January of 2020, I was just installed into the New York State Association of REALTORS leadership team. Just a couple of months later, we were in a full-blown pandemic. I feel if we have the tools and insight Coni provides, the outcome could save lives. Everyone can benefit from this book. This is the kind of book that should be read and shared."

Jennifer Vucetic
Broker/Owner EXIT Realty Empire Associates

TABLE OF CONTENTS

**This book is dedicated to the AWESOME team
that showed up and supported the launching of the
Crisis Knowledge Management and Preparedness
Foundation. (CKMP)**

Known as: BePreparedBeReady.org

*Their tireless efforts and commitment to the vision of
reaching 30 million people have created a movement
that will save lives, property, and money. You know
you are doing something right when the right people,
resources, and opportunities show up to create reality
from a vision.*

*Thank you to all of you who have said yes! Especially,
Deb Hernandez, our Executive Director, and Courtney
Strajen, Operations Director for stepping up and
helping with the enormous amount of work that needs
to be done to launch a nonprofit. Together with our
board and advisory members, we are helping people be
more sustainable, better prepared, and ready when the
unthinkable happens. Without your dedication, none of
what we have created would be possible.*

*All of you have created a legacy that will live on beyond
us. Thank you from the bottom of my heart!*

Coni Meyers, LMC, CBLC, CDC

FORWARD

At 5:14am on New Years Day 2024, my phone buzzed with news of a devastating earthquake in Japan. That is how our year started. Over the last few years many disasters, both natural and accidental have devastated people's lives, property, and sense of security.

I met Coni Meyers years ago through a mutual acquaintance. What followed was an intriguing discussion about preparing the world for the impact of crises and disasters. Since then, I have joined Coni's crusade of preparing individuals, families, and communities to weather crises and recovery hope by joining the board of her CKM Preparedness Foundation. Coni's extensive experience in crisis management training uniquely prepared her to write the first edition of this book. Upon reading it, I shared with her that although it danced around many important topics of financial accounts, estates, and legacy planning, (topics I and my colleagues deal with daily) I felt the book would benefit from addressing some of these matters more directly and clearly.

It has been a pleasure helping Coni work on the third edition of this book and adding some of my extensive experience in working with thousands of financial professionals and attorneys within my firm to the recommendations included here. We hope the recommendations from this book will prepare families, businesses, and individuals for both personal and widespread crisis events, which can and will affect us all at some point in life.

Sir. J. Glen Wagstaff, Esq

INTRODUCTION

In March of 2020, we entered a time of isolation, anxiety, stress, and fear as a result of COVID. However, it also became a time of renewal and hope with the opportunity to realign our lives. I wish to dedicate this book to the millions worldwide who have lost their lives to this pandemic and all who grieve for them.

As a former FEMA inspector and trainer for seven years, I have witnessed many disasters, including hurricanes, earthquakes, typhoons, fires, floods, tsunamis, and countless others. Although it was my first experience with a pandemic, the one thing that can be said is that the process of preparedness, survival, and recovery is pretty much the same, no matter the type of disaster one goes through. There may be some minor differences, but you are prepared for most of them when you are prepared for one. The information you will learn in this book can be applied to your personal life, business, and/or community.

One of the most important things that I want you to take away from this book is that there are gifts and opportunities to be discovered during a disaster's survival and recovery phases. I would encourage you to read my book, *Crystalline Moments,* to learn how to identify these important moments of clarity and understand their significance. We all have thoughts and small and large events that happen in life that can reveal "crystalline moments". COVID is a large event that has affected lives worldwide. We will not know for some time all the gifts and opportunities from this event. One thing to keep in mind, there is always chaos before the gifts and opportunities reveal themselves. I can assure you that once this disaster is over and the recovery phase begins, you will start to see the gifts and opportunities.

Although it was sad to witness the heartaches and challenges disasters brought, the self-sacrificing spirit of humanity made my job rewarding. Post-disaster many ask themselves, "Why". I believe that such events happen for a reason, to bring humanity closer together. History will tell the whole story of COVID, but for now, reflect on the kindness, compassion, and love expressed by many while enduring so much. These are the gifts, or "crystalline moments," that continue to be revealed by disasters, including COVID.

I am writing this book to equip you with the practical, physical, and mental tools you need when disaster strikes. I had wanted to write this book ever since I completed seven years as a FEMA Inspector and trainer. I believe everything happens when it is supposed to, and while experiencing so much during this pandemic, it felt like the perfect time to realize this dream.

We have a responsibility to be prepared when something happens and do what we can to increase our sustainability and decrease our carbon footprint. We will discuss how disaster intensity and frequency have increased dramatically since 1980 and will continue to do so until we get greenhouse gases under control. We will help you identify what you can do to create a more sustainable life.

It is an honor to have J. Glen Wagstaff, Esq. join me in this third edition with his expansive, worldwide award-winning experience and knowledge in the financial world. Individual and business financial situations are dramatically affected by disasters and other crises so we will also be talking about estate and financial planning and what you need to know to have a sustainable financial future as well.

If you were provided this book, please thank the person who gave it to you because they have given you a gift that will change your life. It is the first step to sustainability, preparedness, and resilience,

Coni Meyers, LMC, CBLC, CDC

****QR Codes at the end of the book
include BONUS items for planning and
implementation!****

CHAPTER 1

FEAR AND PROCRASTINATION

Our first discussion revolves around fear and stress felt when experiencing disasters. All of us experience fear at some point. Fear results from the unknown, and disasters create many unknowns. It is important to not allow fear and the negativity created by it to get in the way of common sense. You must" stay **in the moment"** and set aside the" what-ifs." **STOP WATCHING 24-HOUR NEWS!!!** It is important to be informed but watching disaster reports 24/7 is counter-productive to good health. With COVID, we were told to build our immune systems. Watching continuous news about what is happening increases cortisol levels and reduces the ability of our immune system to fight back.

Dr. Kelly McGonigal's book, *The Upside of Stress*, addresses how our view of stress affects us. She states that if we believe stress is harmful to our health, it will be harmful; however, there is no negative effect if we view stress as a challenge. An athlete is an excellent example of controlled stress. When they are about to enter a game with a challenging opponent or team, they do not panic or faint in fear; instead, they channel stress to motivate them to do their best to win.

Much depends on our mindset when it comes to stress caused by disasters. In the emergency management community, they speak about the resilience of individuals, businesses, communities, infrastructure, and emergency management teams. Having a resilient mindset will keep fear and stress under control. How can you have a resilient mindset? PREPARE! PREPARE! PREPARE!

Take a minute to close your eyes and imagine that suddenly the ground starts to shake violently. What do you do? Or visualize a knock on your door from a law enforcement officer or firefighter telling you that you have 15 minutes to evacuate. What now? Typically, the first thing that happens is your mind goes blank!

First responders understand the importance of preparation and practice to overcome fear by maintaining a resilient mindset. In the face of danger, "mind-blanking" takes over our fight-or-flight response kick in blocking what should be a cool and collected reaction. Instead of panic, you MUST turn that "fight-or-flight" behavior into" tend-and-befriend." By doing so, you will know what the first and following steps you need to take are going to be.

"Preparedness Procrastination" is a common term used in emergency management circles, is one of the biggest problems in dealing with disasters. Statistics on the number of Americans prepared for disasters vary depending on the type of preparedness being discussed. According to a 2020 report by the Institute of Certified Public Accountants, 61% of Americans believe that they will be affected by some type of disaster or major crisis in the next 3-5 years. Only 15-35% have done any preparation, and realistically less than 20% are truly prepared. That number has barely changed since 2020. Being prepared means having emergency kits for everyone, planning for each circumstance so you know what to do when something happens, having drills for each circumstance, and mitigating as much as possible. We also need to understand how our carbon footprint is affecting our risk for disasters and what we can do to be more sustainable. Knowing what types of disasters, natural and man-made is critical. For example, are there any chemical or nuclear power plants near you? Is there a risk of train derailments or water supply risks? All of these things should be looked at and plans put into place to protect your home and business.

According to a survey conducted by The Weather Company in 2022, nearly 40% of Americans have experienced severe weather that damaged their homes or made them evacuate, with one in five happening in the last five years. Additionally, the Urban Institute through its 2022 Household Pulse Survey found that 3.3 million people had been displaced by disasters. Currently, we are experiencing disaster events all across the country including the hottest summer on record. Heat kills more individuals than ALL the other disasters COMBINED.

The nonprofit, First Street Foundation, found that 1 in 4 homes could be considered too high a financial risk to insure due to climate risks. Homeowners are facing

60% to 150% or more increases in insurance costs if they can even get insurance. In addition, what is happening globally is also increasing insurance rates through the reinsurers, so we are all footing the bill no matter where in the world disasters strike.

Even with all the conversation and hype about being prepared, a survey conducted by Cummins Home Standby Generators determined that 75% of people felt they were not prepared. Fifty-two percent wanted more food and water, 47% wanted items such as flashlights, batteries, and phone chargers, and 66% wished they had backup power for their home. Additionally, 51% of survey respondents experienced significant inconveniences and financial setbacks. Fifty-one percent said they had to leave their home to stay at hotels or with family or friends, and 45% of homeowners suffered property damage, with an average cost of $3,743.00.

When you look at the overall average of how prepared Americans are in all areas of preparedness, the number is incredibly low. According to the Centers for Disease Control and Prevention (CDC), 48% of Americans do not have emergency supplies, and 44% do not have first aid kits. Fifty-two percent do not have copies of crucial personal documents. Most say they don't have a formal kit when asked about emergency kits, but they know what they would put into one. And therein lies the problem – by the time a disaster strikes, it is far too late to put the kits together.

The bottom line is that very few Americans have everything needed when something strikes. Many survey findings indicate that 15-17% of Americans are prepared overall. For this book, we will use an average of 16%.

So why is it so difficult for people to be prepared? It is like making a will; people procrastinate because they do not want to think about dying. Even though we all understand that we should be prepared, the idea that a crisis or disaster could happen is overwhelming. In preparing for disasters, it is *necessary* to think about the possibility of a disaster. While living busy lives and handling smaller day-to-day disasters, people put off preparing for something they do not want to "think" about. It is easier to procrastinate than face what needs to be done to be prepared."

How many businesses do you think have a disaster preparedness plan? Unless your business is large, only minimal requirements exist. Things like the evacuation of buildings and knowing the location of fire extinguishers are the extent of most preparation. In most areas, government requirements for disaster preparedness do not exist.

Why should you prepare your business for a disaster if you're a business owner? According to FEMA, the U.S. Department of Labor, and the U.S. Chamber of Commerce, only 40% of small businesses reopen after a disaster, and 25% of them will close within a year.

If small businesses cannot reopen within five days of a disaster, the number that will not reopen their doors jumps to 90%. Similarly, another statistic states that 75% of small businesses, even if they do reopen, are gone after two years without preparedness plans.

Small businesses lose an average of $3,000 per day while closed, while medium-size businesses lose an average of $23,000 per day. Think of the impact on individuals and communities who rely on those businesses. It is critical to be prepared and NOT procrastinate.

So far, we have talked about natural and man-made disasters, but life has many other crises that we need to prepare for as well. Our recent encounter with the pandemic, considered a man-made disaster, has brought awareness to Americans of the real need for wills and other important estate planning documents. Unfortunately, "preparedness procrastination" has hit Americans here as well.

Directions Research completed the Xcelerant Survey in September 2022. They found that 66% of adults do not have an estate plan. They also found that 32% said they just had not gotten around to it and 37% said they didn't feel they had enough money to warrant an estate plan. Another 25% said they didn't know where to start. Less than one-third (30%) did not understand what a durable or healthcare power of attorney was.

They did find that people that had become ill with COVID, were 66% more likely to look into estate planning. Two things to get started with estate planning are:

1. Talk to someone you trust, that has done their estate planning, so you understand what is involved. Many people think it is a bigger task than it is.

Find a financial expert you trust. You are going to be discussing difficult topics like death and taxes so make sure you are comfortable with the attorney you choose. Finding the right attorney can make things much easier. Here is a trusted network of professionals who may be able to help: www.IMPowerEDnetwork.com

CHAPTER 2

DISASTERS – WHAT CHANGED?

There has been a significant increase in the number of disasters, their intensity, and their impact on everyday life. The cost of disasters has also risen dramatically in the last five years. Using figures adjusted for inflation, the numbers are staggering when looking at weather-related federal disasters that exceed 1 billion dollars in costs. If you look at the average between 1980 and 2023, the average cost was $60.5 billion a year (CPI Adjusted). However, when you look at the five-year average between 2019 and 2023, the average was $122.5 billion. In 2022 the cost was $145.0 billion. Thus far, the costs for 2023 are at $94.2 but as of this writing, not all costs are included. An example is the fires in Lahaina. The losses are estimated to be over $20 billion just for that one disaster. These are strictly weather-related disasters; it does not consider earthquakes and other types of disasters.

From 1980 to 2023, the number of annual events costing over a billion dollars (CPI) averaged 8.5. That is up from 7.0 from 1980 to 2020. The annual number of events over a billion dollars from 2016 to 2020 was 16.2. From 2021 to 2023 the average was 22 over a billion dollars per year. That more than doubles the number of events in recent years.

According to the US Drought Monitor (USDM), drought covered 55.5% of the US in December 2022 which was the main cause for over 7 million acres to burn. The "megadrought" in the southwest has persisted for the past 22 years and is considered the worst since at least 800 A.D. (1200 years ago). This is according to the journal *Nature Climate Change*.

Until 2020, the most expensive disaster in the U.S. was Hurricane Katrina in 2005 at $162 billion.

The three primary reasons for weather-related disaster increases:

Exposure - higher development and value at risk for possible loss. We have seen more land development in highly desirable and more expensive coastal areas, which come with a higher risk.

Vulnerability – increased weather intensity has resulted in more damage. For example, winds and floodwaters have significantly increased over the last few years.

Climate change - increased frequency of extreme weather-related disasters. Scientists state that if we do not get greenhouse gasses under control by 2030, it could be irreversible. Even if greenhouse gases are controlled, they say it will take 25-40 years to reverse the effects. We need to look at our carbon footprint and do our part to reduce the greenhouse gases we are emitting.

Man-made Disaster Increases

While natural disasters have increased annually, so have man-made disasters.

COVID cost the US an estimated $13 Trillion during the first 20 weeks of the pandemic. The estimated cumulative financial costs are estimated at more than $16 trillion.

Gun Violence Archive tracks mass shootings. Between 2019 and 2020 mass shootings jumped from 414 to 610. Then 2021 became the worst year thus far with 689. In 2022, there were 647 incidents including 51 school shootings. In 2023 there were 656 incidents recorded with 82 school shootings. .

According to the FBI's Internet Crime Report, Americans lost over $12.5 billion to cybercrime in 2023. That is a 22% increase from the previous year. According to Cybersecurity Ventures, cybercrime costs the world $8 trillion in 2023. That is projected to increase to $10.5 trillion by 2025.

Insurance, Mortgage, and Other Financial Costs

Whether we are talking about natural or man-made disasters the financial costs of disasters are staggering.

As climate change increases the frequency and severity of disasters, insurance companies are scrambling to adjust rates or are deciding to pull out of states altogether. One in four homes is now considered too high a risk for insurance. Without insurance, there cannot be a mortgage. Without the ability to have a mortgage, property values will decrease. Since most state laws do not allow insurance companies to base their insurance rates on future risks, insurance companies and government agencies are scrambling to find a way to address the problem. Most insurance companies are paying out more in claims than they are bringing in from premiums. In addition, it is no longer just states with hurricanes and wildfires, like the southern and western states, but states all across the country. Tornados, drought, freezing, severe winter, and summer storms do not discriminate. They are happening everywhere.

Over the last 5 years, insurance premiums have risen by 33.8% with some areas experiencing increases as high as 60% We are already seeing where homeowners are not able to afford insurance.

Insurance companies are leading the way when it comes to innovative ways to reduce greenhouse gases. Insurance companies are actively supporting the net-zero transition by ensuring capital expenditures related to low-carbon technologies and creating risk transfer solutions for climate-related risks. They collaborate using data-driven methods and making sure everyone knows about the risks related to climate change. Many offer incentives to their clients and employees through programs that promote lifestyle changes to decrease greenhouse gases.

All of this has a major effect on American's financial situation then add to that the inadequate emergency savings people have to protect themselves and this is a formula for financial disaster.

According to the 2023 Savings Report by Bankrate, more than one in five Americans have no emergency savings. It is recommended that we have at least 3 months of emergency expenses saved. In 2023 30% had saved some emergency money but not the 3 months recommended.

Saving for emergencies is the number one goal of Americans although less than half would be able to cover a $1000 emergency expense.

Here are 3 tips for building your emergency fund:

1. Figure out how much you need in emergency savings
2. Open a savings account just for emergencies
3. Make a budget around savings

Creating an emergency expense savings account will give you the resiliency to build back when disasters or crises happen. It is generally recommended to have a minimum of 3-6 months' worth of income or expenses saved for these moments. Don't let "preparedness procrastination" prevail.

Hopefully, the information presented thus far will move you to protect yourself, your family, your business, and your community.

CHAPTER 3

HOW PREPARED ARE YOU?

Being prepared will potentially save your life and reduce the cost of recovery. The three components to being prepared for disasters are the *why*, the *what*, and the *when*.

When you understand the *why*, you will find the starting point for being prepared. You will also understand the importance of having a resilient mindset and how it will affect the outcome when a disaster strikes. Additionally, you will realize how being prepared helps you react immediately and the importance of being self-sufficient, as it may take 24-48 hours before first responders can reach you.

What do you need to have to be prepared? It starts with the basics - your emergency kits and your plans. It is critical to have a list of everything you need to take and understand how important it is to pay attention to emergency alerts. Once you have the basics, you can then look at what additional items should go into the kits depending on the disaster risks in your area.

Additionally, having the right financial products and the right legal documents will give you options, security, and the ability to enforce your rights and wishes in stressful and potentially devastating situations.

When to prepare? ***Before*** a disaster, not while the disaster is happening. This ***will*** save lives. It has been proven that those prepared will recover faster than those that are not. Preparedness will simplify what you need to do and help you avoid the domino effects of secondary crises that can occur when you are not prepared legally, financially, or otherwise.

Where do you start? **Mindset!** When you ask victims of disasters and first responders, they will tell you that your mindset is the most important component of preparing for, surviving, and recovering from a disaster. Your mindset is what keeps you from being disoriented and immobile. A resilient mindset is most important as it not only allows you to bounce back but bounce back better than before the disaster happened.

CHAPTER 4

RESILIENCE IN DISASTER

In an interview, Dr. Alia Crum, Assistant Professor of Psychology at Stanford University, explained how a mindset is a lens through which you view the world. The mindset we choose plays a dramatic role in shaping the psychological and physiological effects on attention, arousal, motivation, and affect. There are many types of mindsets: resilient, stressful, challenging, survival, fixed, growth, and persistence, to name a few. When it relates to disasters, a resilient mindset is by far the most important.

In emergency management circles, the resilience of communities, businesses, and individuals is a hot topic. First responders will tell you that the most important factor in how one prepares, survives, and recovers from a disaster depends entirely on a person's mindset. Resilience is defined as 'the ability to recover quickly from difficulty'.

Why is a resilient mindset so important when it comes to disasters? Usually, the first thing that happens in an emergency is that the mind goes blank; it figuratively freezes. When we believe we have an intruder in the house or that our car has been stolen, we ask ourselves, "What do I do now?" Fear and panic can take control, and a person will go into a fight-or-flight response.

One of my interviewees from my 'Kickbutt Leadership Interview Series' has a real estate office with 40 agents in Malibu, California. Sarah was born there, and her mother still lived in their family home. During the Malibu wildfires in 2017, her mother's home was burned to the ground. Many of her agents also had homes that were damaged or destroyed.

Sarah, her husband, and 2 little girls lived a short distance from her mom but felt they were safe as the fire going the opposite direction away from their home. In the middle of the night, they got a knock on the door, and when she answered, it was a fireman letting her know that she and her family had only 15 minutes to evacuate. Mind you, this is a highly intelligent, confident businesswoman. She closed the door and hit the panic button. She spent 5 minutes spinning in a circle, trying to figure out what to take. She and her family arrived at the shelter only to discover that they had not brought anything for her girls. As I was talking with her, it was clear that this still caused her anguish.

During a conversation with a fire chief, who headed the Los Angeles County Community Emergency Response Team (CERT) he shared that he found it difficult to remain in control when he learned that a fire was headed toward his neighborhood. His training and resilience helped him overcome his fear and be able to perform effectively.

When prepared with a plan, you will know what to do and where you should go. Without preparation, there is chaos. With preparation, there is resilience. Take a brief look at what happened when COVID spread across the U.S. There was a run-on toilet paper, hand sanitizer, water, and food supplies. Most Americans were not prepared, and panic ensued.

In emergency management, resilience means more than "bouncing back." It means re-evaluating plans after a disaster and determining what needs to change to mitigate or lessen the risk of a future disaster. It means rebuilding better than before. A resilient mindset will ask, 'How can we reduce the risk? How can we do a better job of building back?'

Resilient preparedness is planning and training. Resilient survival is responsiveness and efficiency. Resilient recovery is the ability to see a better outcome and rebuild better than before.

How do you build a resilient mindset when preparing for the unknown? Here are six tips for embracing resiliency. You will turn resilience into a mindset for change by following these tips. (BTW, these will work in any part of your life.)

> **S.T.O.P.** An acronym used in emergency management and first responders: Stop, Think, Observe, and Plan. Jon Kabat-Zinn, the creator

of the Stress Reduction Clinic and the Center for Mindfulness in Medicine, Health Care and Society at the University of Massachusetts Medical School, also developed a similar mindfulness practice called S.T.O.P. By practicing S.T.O.P., you create focus and remain centered, thus allowing you to become resilient. This is a great acronym for all parts of your life and business.

Stop- Allow your mind to go completely blank.

Take deep breaths Breathe in through the nose and out through the mouth. This allows your mind to become calm and focused.

Observe- Observe what you are feeling inside and calm any fears through breathing then observe what is happening around you. You will know then how to proceed

Proceed- You enact your plan; and move forward with confidence. Resilience leads to persistence.

In addition to S.T.O.P. – Stay in a resilient mindset

These additional four things will help you change the chemistry of your brain so you can stay resilient and move forward. Practice them once in the morning and again in the evening.

Being grateful- Find 3 things to be grateful for and write them down.

Celebrating your successes. Even if it is just getting out of bed. If you are putting together your emergency kits and plans celebrate as each is completed. If in survival mode, celebrate that no one was hurt or that you survived and that your home or other possessions can be replaced or rebuilt.

See the beauty. I call life-changing moments "crystalline moments." Crystalline means sparkly or clear, so moments of clarity. In any "crystalline moment," there is always a gift or opportunity. Look around you and find the gift or opportunity in your situation.

Believe that you can recover. Create a vision for the outcome, and the vision will become a reality. You cannot go toward a vision, you must come from the vision, and to come from a vision, you must become the vision. By creating a vision and having a resilient mindset, you will succeed.

A resilient mindset is essential in any scenario.

CHAPTER 5

MAKE PLANS TODAY

The month of September is National Preparedness Month. By having a disaster preparedness plan when the time comes, you will know what you need to do, how you need to do it, and when you need to do it.

Let's talk about the emergency kit first. You need to have a kit for your home, car, and work/business locations. Each member of your household should have their own kit. One for each child, seniors, and members with disabilities.

In addition to your regular emergency kit, you need to have small go-kits that only contain essentials if there is not enough time or space to take your entire kit.

For example, you cannot take a full-size duffle bag when rescued by boat. Each member of the household should have a go-kit that can be a part of their emergency kit.

Our first initiative through CKMP is called Kits4Kids. We have designed special go-kits for kids that can be velcroid to the bottom of a kid's everyday backpack. It can go everywhere that backpack goes and provides them with some basic protection. When there is a need for their emergency kit the go-kit comes out of the everyday backpack and into their emergency kit. The go-kit provides approximately 40% of what goes into an emergency kit. To learn more about Kits4Kids:

The basic items in an emergency kit are pretty much the same for each kit, whether for the home, car, or work; however, there may be a few different items depending on the risk factors in the area.

Do not forget *cash*! One of the easily overlooked things is putting cash in a kit. Think about how much cash you will need. Imagine if the ATMs are not working, the electricity is out, and you cannot get cash from a store. A good rule of thumb would be enough cash for a week in a hotel, food, gas, and miscellaneous.

Other items to consider are photos, heirlooms, and other irreplaceable items. If the item is too large for the emergency kit have a plan of what to do with it. When I was doing FEMA inspections, people often relayed that losing their photos was the most difficult material loss. Many people put pictures in boxes and then store them in a closet or under the bed on the floor. In the event of a flood, they will be irreparably damaged or destroyed.

If you have ever lost pictures from a smartphone, you know how devastating it is. Second, digitize them and store them on an external hard drive or upload them to the cloud. I suggest, if you can, keeping your external hard drive and/or vintage photos with the emergency kit so that they go with you in an evacuation.

Dave Ramsey recommends creating a legacy drawer in which all your important documents, pictures, and sentimental items are found easily in the event of an emergency. The key is to be able to find and run with your most important belongings in a matter of minutes without having to think about what is important enough to hunt down.

One of the first disasters I worked on was a flood in Central California. I pulled up to the front of the home, and an older man was sitting on his front steps weeping. He was holding what appeared to be just a bunch of old wood. When I asked him about the wood, he shared with me that the pieces of wood had been his grandfather's toolbox. Preparing will move you to a plan to protect those items.

Items to have in an emergency kit include:

- Cash
- Water - 1 gallon per person for 3-5 days
- Food - Non-perishable food for 3-5 days, including infant formula and pet food

- Battery-powered radio or NOAA weather radio
- Flashlight and whistle
- Documents - family and other important papers, especially powers of attorney (copied and stored in the cloud)
- Dust masks, plastic sheeting, and duct tape
- Moist towelettes, trash bags, and plastic ties for personal sanitation
- A few basic tools (pliers, screwdriver, wrench, etc.)
- Local map, paper, and pen
- Cellphone with charger, car charger, solar charger, and/or portable power bank
- Prescriptions and an extra pair of glasses
- Fire extinguisher, stormproof matches
- Emergency reference material obtained from the local planning office
- Sleeping bags, clothing, sturdy shoes
- Household items, such as paper supplies, bleach, and a medicine dropper
- Feminine hygiene products or other special needs for household members such as diapers for infants
- Games, books, puzzles

Once your home kit is complete, focus on creating emergency kits for each household member and then kits for your car and workplace or business. Be sure to evaluate the specific needs of those in your household, especially older adults and people with disabilities. Once a year, be sure to refresh your emergency kits. Take out items with an expired date or no longer necessary and replace items borrowed from the kits.

CHAPTER 6

CREATE A PLAN

Next, it is time to create your plans. Several different types of plans need to be considered. Let us start with emergency alerts and warnings. If you have not already signed up to receive these alerts, you should do so now.

The Integrated Public Alert and Warning System, or IPAWS, is a national system for local alerting that provides authenticated emergency alerts and life-saving information messaging to the public through TV, radio, and mobile devices. It was created to unify and modernize the United States' Emergency Alert System, National Warning System, Wireless Emergency Alerts, and the NOAA (National Oceanic and Atmospheric Administration) Weather Radio.

Decide which devices you will have this information on. When a disaster is imminent, these alerts will provide you with instructions on what to do. Now, ask yourself:

- What are the unique needs of my family?
- What is my parent's plan?
- What is my kid's plan?
- What is my estate plan?
- What is my shelter plan?

- What is my pet plan?
- What are my evacuation routes?
- What is my family/household communication plan?
- What is my business emergency plan?
- What is my staff and team member communication plan?

Consider the unique needs of each household member. Some things to consider are prescriptions, special medical devices, glasses, etc.

The parent plan is the plan for each adult in the household. What will you/they do if at home? At work? And what about the kids? Are they at home, school, a babysitter's, or a friend's home? What are they to do in each of those scenarios?

You should also make plans for your pet(s), as most shelters will not accept them. In every disaster, pets are left behind to fend for themselves under dire circumstances. First responders spend countless hours rescuing these helpless family members. And hundreds of others work to provide food and shelter for them. As an inspector, it was heartbreaking when animals were found. I implore you, **PLEASE DO NOT LEAVE YOUR PETS BEHIND!** Make sure that they have their kit and that you know where they are going.

Often, as in my friend's example in Malibu, you only have minutes to leave. Learn where the nearest shelter is located so that you are not in the dark about where to go. Know where the closest shelter is if you are at work. The same goes for your family members. If you are separated, everyone needs to know where the nearest shelter they need to go is. Do practice drills, driving to the shelter using several different routes. It is important to have at least two routes you can take. You will learn how to get there and how long it will take.

It is important to know another route to get out when you need to leave. In Santa Barbara, CA, there is one main route out of town – Highway 101. The southbound lane was closed during their notorious wildfires because of an overturned truck.

This book does not detail a business emergency and continuity plan but that is an integral part of your planning if you have a business. As we stated earlier, 75% percent of businesses without a plan will not be in business after two years. You will find a list of things to consider in a plan in the QR code at the end of this book.

You should also prepare your business with effective succession planning to ensure continuity if a personal crisis, such as the death, incapacity, or absence of owners or key individuals in the business should occur. This can be done through guidance from competent legal counsel and often includes financial considerations which can and should be built into your succession planning. If you are looking for qualified professionals to orient you in this type of planning, you can find a list of them at www.IMPowerEDnetwork.com.

When it comes to financial resiliency, having proper beneficiary designations on accounts and adequate funding of a trust plan are crucial aspects of estate planning. They can help ensure that your assets are distributed efficiently, according to your wishes, while minimizing costs, delays, and potential tax implications. It is advisable to consult with legal and financial professionals to create and maintain an estate plan that aligns with your goals and provides for the needs of your loved ones.

The benefits include:

- Asset distribution according to your wishes
- Avoiding probate
- Privacy and confidentiality
- Minimizing estate taxes
- Flexibility and control

It is important to have some basic estate planning documents that are critical to have completed including:

- Financial powers of attorney
- Medical directives
- Healthcare powers of attorney

- Last will and testaments
- Revocable living trusts

Next PRACTICE! PRACTICE! PRACTICE! Run drills with the entire family and/or business a minimum of twice a year. Review the plans once a year to ensure they are up to date.

CHAPTER 7

MAKE A LIST

Make a thorough list of the inventory in your kit so that when you review the kit, you know exactly what should be in it—for example, photos, pet information, and heirlooms. Your list should include your plans and important documents organized in a fireproof/waterproof drawer or box, to make it easy to grab and run. Include what is to be done with the items in your kit if you cannot take them. Do not forget to make copies and put them on an external hard drive and the cloud.

Some of the documents you should have copies of include:

- Driver's licenses
- Deeds
- Wills
- Medical, home, car, and life insurance information
- Medical records
- Passports
- Social Security cards
- Birth certificates
- Personal contacts
- Family immunizations

- Pets' medical records
- Bank Account information
- Credit card information
- Recent tax returns
- Homeownership documents
- Rental or lease agreements
- Video and inventory of household and valuable possessions
- Living will
- Power of attorney documents
- Marriage certificates
- Custody agreements
- Trust documents
- Education records
- Professional licenses
- Employment contracts
- List of online accounts and passwords
- Family emergency plan with designated meeting places and contacts
- Evacuation routes and shelter information
- Social media accounts and contact information
- Any other documents specific to your situation or needs
- Corporate documents
- List of domain names, email addresses, and other online information
- Create a password management application with instructions on how to access the passwords

You may want to consider having a "legacy drawer" where all of these documents along with other instructions can be stored.

Additional things you may want to consider are special instructions on how things around the home operate, i.e. how to light the pilot light or how to set the sprinkler systems. Funeral instructions, how to pay certain bills and any personal messages, even videos Include instructions of what all is in the drawer and how it is organized.

IMPORTANT! I can promise that you will not remember everything you own. Take videos of the inside and outside of your home. Go room by room, with cabinets and drawers open, so you have documentation of everything you own. Make sure this recording is stored somewhere in addition to your home and stored in the cloud. Items not covered by insurance may be assessed for special tax deductions.

CHAPTER 8

BEFORE, DURING & AFTER DISASTERS

BEFORE - put your kits, plans, and lists together. *Next* - run family and business drills; if feasible, create a minimum of two ways to get out of each room. Drive evacuation routes, so the entire household knows the routes. Maintain and upgrade your emergency kits and plans on an annual basis. Know your company's disaster plan.

NOW - practice **S.T.O.P.** Stop, Think, Observe, and Plan. Stop, and take three breaths to gather your thoughts. Think, what is your current situation? Observe what you are feeling (your *inner* voice tells you what needs to happen next). Plan, you made them, and now it is time to use them.

DURING - *first*, **S.T.O.P.** Take 2 minutes to clear your mind and become resilient. Now the planning and practice kick in, and resilience follows, negating panic. Gather your emergency kits and plans and do what you are told to do by the authorities. (You will hear me say this several times!!)   **Do Not** put yourself, your loved ones, volunteers, and first responders at risk. As a former FEMA inspector, I can promise you it is not worth it!

Help your family to **S.T.O.P.** so that they are present and not paralyzed. If you need to find shelter, do that before anything else.

During the Santa Barbara wildfires, people were told to evacuate, and most did. The fires were put out, and residents returned to their homes. A few days later, some were told again to evacuate due to the potential of mudslides. Some refused to follow that directive resulting in the death of twenty-nine people, three of whom were never found. The name for this phenomenon is "Evacuation Fatigue". **IT CAN NOT BE EMPHASIZED ENOUGH THAT WHEN TOLD TO EVACUATE, DO IT!**

AFTER - Secure your property as best you can. If there is damage, do **not** begin clean-up or remove anything until you take photos of what is broken or destroyed, and save **all** expense receipts to present to the insurance adjuster. If something unsafe or critical needs to be removed, do that after taking a photo. Once your situation is stable, contact all the appropriate agencies for help. There is a list later in this book.

CHAPTER 9

LEADERSHIP

What is disaster leadership? It is the difference between a speedy recovery and one that is difficult or impossible. In a household and a business, each person should be evaluated for their strengths and weaknesses to determine their role. Certain skill sets are critical when it comes to disasters and leadership. If you panic easily and find it difficult to be decisive or solve a problem, you may not be the right person to take charge.

It is important to be a good observer of yourself and those around you who may be feeling traumatized or highly charged emotionally. It is critically important to identify those individuals and address their needs as soon as possible.

Author Stephen King says, "There is no harm in hoping for the best as long as you are prepared for the worst." In a disaster situation, this is an absolute truth. The person taking charge will determine what changes may be needed in the recovery phase and make good solid decisions based on the situation. They will start with where they are and what they have right now and move forward. They will determine the first step that needs to be taken, and then take that step.

Leadership With Children

Time to talk about how children are affected and how to reduce stress. Know that it is **_not_** the words you speak but the body language and tonality being used that will have the most significant impact.

In the planning phase, have an authentic conversation with them about what might happen. Let them be a part of the planning. During a disaster, stay calm so they too will stay calm. Allowing them to help with the preparation will give them a better understanding of what is going on and what comes next. If everything is shared, much of the fear will be minimized. If you need to evacuate, let them bring a personal item that will give them comfort and make them feel safe, such as a teddy bear or blanket. The Kits4Kids will help to provide a sense of peace of mind for the kids and their parents.

Be careful what you say to others if children are present because what they hear may be understood differently from what you mean. Be present and available for them. Frequently ask them questions to find out what they are thinking and feeling. This is especially important once the recovery has started. If children act out and are not sleeping or eating, it may be important to seek professional help. When you allow children to be a part of planning and recovery, they are less worried about the future.

Leadership With Your Business

Perhaps you have a thriving business with over 100 employees. Your company is incredibly successful because of your sales and marketing leadership skills. The leadership skills that helped you become successful may not be the leadership skills that are needed in a disaster. You are more likely to be good at relationship building (which is important in a disaster), but your organizational and project management skills may not be sufficient. Find that person who makes a good project manager to lead during a disaster. A swift recovery comes down to rolling out the plans, making the adjustments, and staying on track with what needs to be done.

CHAPTER 10

COMMUNICATION

Communication is KEY in a disaster and is another component of a speedy recovery. A strong communication plan is critical. Everyone in the household and/or business must understand the communication plan. Create a call tree and practice the communication plan so that everyone understands their responsibilities.

Everyone should have an accurate, updated list of all necessary phone numbers and know who they will need to call. Make sure to have contacts outside of your area in case communication is down. Having family or friends that everyone can call is vital if you cannot reach one another.

Involve your children, so they understand the importance of being prepared. All children should learn how to call 911 and relate their emergency. Keep a list of updated, all-important phone numbers on the refrigerator or other conspicuous spot, so they are prepared to call for help. Have a list in their backpacks or cell phones in the event they are at school or someone else's home. A great solution for kids is the Kits4Kids so they always have emergency numbers and safety items with them. Run family drills to practice the communication plan.

Have an intermediary, a relative or friend, outside your immediate area that everyone in the emergency area can call to relay information regarding their safety and well-being.

If evacuated, communicate to others where you will be staying. The reverse is also true; when you leave the shelter to return home, make sure to let others know that you are returning. Include a solar charging unit or portable power bank in your kit to maintain communication with others. Be prepared with battery-operated radios to listen to instructions from authorities.

When communicating with one another, be as present as possible, so everyone remains calm and stress-free. Researchers have found that approximately 90% of us are not good listeners. When it comes to disasters, listening skills are critical. Listen to instructions from authorities, listen to one another carefully, so things are heard correctly, and listen to your children carefully to understand their needs. Watch their body language and tonality to pick up on anything they may not be saying, but that could be a warning sign. Allow children to communicate with grandparents or others they love, which will aid in their return to normalcy.

Communication is 55% body language, 38% tonality, and 7% spoken word. Listening is more than hearing words; it is about paying attention to what is not being said. Our minds are usually thinking about what we are going to say before the other person has finished or about something entirely different than what is being conveyed. When it comes to disasters, listening can be the difference between surviving and perishing.

Here are 10 steps to good listening:

> **Step 1:** Face the speaker and maintain eye contact
> **Step 2:** Be attentive but relaxed
> **Step 3:** Keep an open mind
> **Step 4:** Listen to the words and try to picture what is being said
> **Step 5:** Do not interrupt or impose your "solutions"
> **Step 6:** Wait for the speaker to pause before asking clarifying questions
> **Step 7:** Ask questions only to ensure understanding
> **Step 8:** Try to feel what the speaker is feeling
> **Step 9:** Give the speaker regular feedback
> **Step 10:** Pay attention to what is *not* said

CHAPTER 11

DISASTER TYPES

Disasters can be classified as natural or man-made. Their impact on countless lives can be catastrophic, physically and mentally. Many individuals who experience a disaster develop post-traumatic stress disorder and depression. It is estimated that as many as 50% of people experiencing a major disaster will require some form of clinical psychological care. The overwhelming loss can leave people too paralyzed to do anything.

Economically, it may be almost impossible to recover. The environmental impact may alter ecosystems and change the livability of an area. The cost of insurance may be unaffordable or not available. Preparedness for each potential disaster is the answer to mitigating as much risk as possible.

Disasters of all types have a major effect on property values. Having multiple types of disasters in a short period can have a lasting effect on market values. Homes located in areas of repeated fire or flooding will experience serious devaluation. There may be rezoning that will reduce the size of the property or the ability to rebuild at all. Coastline properties that may have an increased risk of flooding, landslides, or storm damage will not be as desirable as they once were.

Following a disaster, appraisers are called upon to determine the value of a partially damaged or destroyed home. Even if a disaster does not impact a home, the value can be significantly affected due to the surrounding damage. It isn't easy to find comps for such a neighborhood. How do you figure out the value of a home that no longer exists?

Insurance also plays a factor in home values. Many homeowners are forced into foreclosure because of *inadequate insurance*. According to Frank Nothaft, Executive, Chief Economist for CoreLogic®, "The disruption of a family's regular flow of income and payments, as well as substantial loss in property value, can trigger mortgage default; especially if homeowners are underinsured and cannot afford to rebuild."

Climate change has profoundly impacted the real estate industry and will continue to affect safety and property values as global warming increases. It is important to understand climate change's effect on our communities and surrounding areas as a consumer. It is wise to know what questions to ask when purchasing a home. The following statement is from the article, "Selling Real Estate in the Era of Disaster", from the March 7 issue of *REALTOR® Magazine."* In recent years we have seen polar vortexes cause 60-degree temperature swings from one day to the next, which can be detrimental to homes' plumbing, electrical, and other systems. The new reality is that the country must contend with increasingly violent climate events, and business owners who live and work in disaster-prone areas are likely to experience more disruption to their businesses."

Once there is a disaster in an area, obtaining a mortgage becomes more difficult due to possible mitigations of future disasters. Insurance rates go up or may not be available. As we stated earlier, one in four homes is considered too high a risk to insure. To completely understand the risk, get involved with your community and participate in the preparation. It all goes back to community mitigation and preparation to lower potential disasters' impact on any area. Fannie Mae and Freddie Mac are now evaluating options regarding climate change that could make a huge difference in whether a mortgage will be made available and under what guidelines.

BePreparedBeReady.org offers education for individuals, businesses, and communities that details all the natural and man-made disasters and more detailed recommendations on preparing, surviving, and recovering from disasters. In this book, I will be covering the following types of disasters: house and wildfires, floods, earthquakes, hurricanes, landslides and mudflows, winter storms, tornados and summer storms, and droughts. To find out more use QR Code at the end of the book.

Let's start with understanding the difference between a weather watch and a warning in considering natural disasters.

Watches are issued 6-12 hours before a severe weather situation. They typically cover a wide area that is prime for severe weather. They have the potential to damage property and threaten the lives of people. Have a plan in case the watch develops into a warning.

Warnings are issued when severe weather is imminent or is already occurring. Typically, they cover a smaller area and last approximately 30-60 minutes for short periods. ***Take immediate cover or action***.

Each type of threat has its criteria to meet the term "severe," but keep your list, including your plans and stocked emergency kit close at hand in all disasters.

At the point of evacuation, no matter what kind of disaster it is, when told to leave, do not ask questions and do not discuss with your neighbors whether they are going… **DO IT**. People lose their lives because they refuse to evacuate. In virtually every disaster, first responders and volunteers put their lives at risk to save those who thought they could outwit Mother Nature.

You may have heard this story: A man received an alert that a river was about to spill over and flood his town and that people should evacuate. He assured himself and said, "I'm a religious man. My God will save me." As the waters rose and started covering the first floor, a boat of rescuers came by to take the man to safety. But the man replied, "I'm a religious man. My God will save me." As the waters continued to rise, the man sought out safety on the roof. Shortly after, a helicopter came hovering overhead, and a rescuer shouted down, "I'm dropping this ladder and will take you to safety." The man replied, "I'm a religious man. My God will save me." The waters continued to rise, and the man drowned. Standing before his god, he said, "I'm a religious man. I thought you would save me. Why did this happen?" His god replied, "I sent you an alert, a boat, AND a helicopter. What more did you expect?"

PLEASE LEAVE WHEN YOU ARE TOLD.

House Fires

In as little as 30 seconds, a small flame can turn into a major fire. In five minutes, a residence can be engulfed in flames. It takes only a few minutes for a home to fill with black smoke and toxic gases, which can cause disorientation and drowsiness. Death by asphyxiation exceeds burns by three to one. Save your local fire department's emergency number on your cell phone. Be sure to create an escape plan, especially one to address the evacuation needs of older adults and people with disabilities.

There is an average of 358,500 house fires each year.

- 50% start in the kitchen
- 7% start in the bedroom
- 6% start in the chimney
- 4% start in the living room
- 3% start in the laundry room

Whether it is your home or business, practice fire drills to ensure everyone knows how to get out of the building quickly. These drills should include _feeling_ your way out and two exits from each room. If there are screens on the windows, everyone should know how to get them off quickly. How will someone safely get out of the window on a second story or higher? Establish two locations where everyone is to meet once they are safe. Make sure to include children in your drills. Have them listen to the fire and carbon monoxide detectors, so they know what to do if it goes off.

If your clothes catch fire, **_DO NOT RUN!_** _Drop_ to the ground, _cover_ your face with your hands, and _roll_ over and over until the fire is out. If you cannot drop and roll, wrap yourself in a blanket or towel to smother the flames. Use cool water (not cold) to immediately treat a burn as the heat will continue to cook the flesh. Cover with a clean, dry cloth and seek medical treatment right away. Everyone must know to STOP, DROP, and ROLL if their clothes catch fire.

Check your fire and carbon monoxide detectors frequently to ensure they function properly. Fire detectors should be replaced every 8-10 years and batteries tested monthly. Replace the batteries annually unless using non-replaceable 10-year lithium batteries. There should be smoke/carbon monoxide detectors on every house level, especially inside and outside bedrooms.

During a fire, dark toxic smoke accumulates first at the ceiling; therefore, crawl low and under this cloud. Before opening a door, feel the knob and door to see if they are hot. If they are, use your second escape route to get away. If you cannot get to someone needing assistance, get out and call 911 and tell them where the person is located. If pets are trapped, let the firefighters know right away. If unable to exit a burning building, close the door and cover the vents and cracks around the doors with wet blankets, towels, or other cloth material, to keep gases out. Call 911 and let them know where you are. Go to a window with a cloth or a flashlight to signal where you are. If there is more than one window in the room, keep the other windows shut except the one where you are signaling for help. If in an office building or high-rise, **DO NOT USE AN ELEVATOR!**

Before a fire or other disaster, provide information to your local fire station about any older adults or people with disabilities and what their needs may be. Be sure to include their location in the home.

Wildfires

Wildfires can flare up and travel quickly. They can move up to 6-14 mph, which can be faster than the average person who runs 10 mph. It is critical to be prepared if you live in an area with a potential risk. Sign up for your community's emergency alert system on your cell phone. Know your local evacuation routes and have at least two ways to escape. Do not forget your emergency kit, which should include N95 respirator masks, your pets, and your pet's emergency kit.

Remove flammable materials, debris, and dead vegetation within 100 feet of your property. If you have grass, immediately clean up trimmings after mowing. Use fire-resistant materials when building, renovating, or making repairs to your home. Look at the possibility of retrofitting the roof and siding with fire-resistant materials. Keep important documents in a fireproof box with backup copies stored on an external hard drive and in the cloud. **Review your property insurance with your insurance agent to ensure you are properly covered**. According to insurance industry experts, about 60% of all homes are underinsured.

When the authorities tell you to evacuate, **DO SO IMMEDIATELY!** If trapped, call 911 to let authorities know where you are and then **turn on all lights** so they can find you. A response may be delayed or even impossible, which is why it is so critical to evacuate when you are told to. *No property is worth your life or that of your loved ones*.

Floods

Of all disasters, floods are the most common. They account for 90% of natural disasters and occur in 99% of all U.S. counties. Flooding is defined as rising water and is **NOT** covered by homeowner's insurance. Only water coming from the sky is covered by a homeowner's policy. If you live in an area classified as a flood zone, you are required to carry flood insurance. You can purchase flood insurance if you live in a low- to moderate-risk area for flooding; however, know that 25% of low to moderate-risk areas will experience repeated flooding.

If you experience a natural disaster and receive money from FEMA for flood damage, then flood insurance will be required in the future for that location. During my time with FEMA, I saw numerous floods in small towns near the top of the mountains.

With climate change, the effect of flooding from dangerous storms, tornadoes, and hurricanes is on the rise. FEMA recently updated its flood maps. You may not have lived initially in a high-risk flood area, but you may now. Check with your local planning office for information about your area. You may want to investigate purchasing flood insurance even if you are not at high risk.

While monitoring for an emergency flood, prepare your home by lifting possessions off the floor and turning off utilities, including electricity, water, and gas. Put sandbags in the toilet and drain hoses to prevent sewage backflow. If there is time, move vehicles, outdoor equipment, chemicals, and toxins to higher locations. When you are under a flood warning, evacuate to your shelter immediately. Know your plan for older adults and people with disabilities, as well as pets.

If it is too late to leave, first and foremost, stay calm. Remember to **S.T.O.P.** and say, "I am/We are safe," or whatever you want the outcome to be.

Do not drive into water of an unknown depth! Cars can float in as little as one foot of water, and two feet of rushing water will carry away an SUV and a pickup truck. If your car is flooded, lower the windows as quickly as possible and escape onto the roof of the vehicle.

Most emergency procedures follow a similar pattern - know your evacuation routes, grab your emergency kit, and find a safe shelter as soon as possible. During floods, do not walk, swim, or drive through floodwaters, and stay off bridges that cross over fast-moving water. Also, avoid drains and waters that are over knee-deep (use a stick to check depth). Move to higher ground or a higher floor, including the roof of your house, until help arrives; however, **NEVER SEEK SHELTER IN AN ATTIC**.

Do not use gas or electrical appliances that have been in floodwater until they have been inspected. Boil tap or other unpotable water until authorities have said it is safe to drink.

Earthquakes

According to research by Statista, between 1974-2003, forty-two states had strong naturally occurring earthquakes of a magnitude of 3.5 or higher. Sixteen of those states had twenty or more, with Alaska having the most at 12,053. California came in second with 4,895. "United States - Number of Strong Earthquakes" To check out your state and the risks of earthquakes: www.statista.com/statistics/203956/number-of-strong-earthquakes-in-the-us-by-state/.)

Studies are currently being conducted to differentiate natural earthquakes from man-made ones. Earthquakes from hydraulic extracting, known as fracking, involve shooting water, sand, and chemicals under high pressure deep into the ground to release oil and gas, which can trigger the movement of faults. Since 2008, there has been a 70% increase in earthquakes in Oklahoma, leaving scientists to believe it is unlikely that all are from natural causes.

During an earthquake, Drop, Cover, and Hold on. You can do many things to protect yourself, others, and your property from damage caused by earthquakes. You can secure heavy objects, cabinet doors, framed photos and art, books and bookcases, mirrors, electronics, filing cabinets, water heaters, refrigerators, and other heavy appliances.

Drop to your hands and knees. Cover your head and neck with arms and, if a table or desk is nearby, go underneath it for shelter. If under a table or desk, hold on with one hand. Do **not** run outside where trees or power lines may fall. Do **not** rely on a door frame. If seated and unable to drop to the floor, bend forward, use your arms to cover your head and neck, and hold until the shaking stops.

DO NOT USE ELEVATORS!

Hurricanes

While there is a debate on whether the annual number of hurricanes is on the rise, it appears that hurricanes' intensity and destruction have increased. In 2020, the National Oceanic and Atmospheric Administration (NOAA) predicted a 60% increase in Atlantic hurricane activity that season.

The Atlantic hurricane season is from June 1st to November 30th. The eastern Pacific hurricane season is from May 15th to November 30th. Forecasts for each season are released in May, which is also Hurricane Preparedness Month. Each year, FEMA has a 7-Day Preparedness Plan for the hurricane season, a perfect reminder to review your preparedness. Know your risk, sign up for the emergency alert system, evaluate your emergency kit, and prepare your plans and documents, including extra cash. Keep a full tank of fuel in your vehicle or fully charge your electric vehicle. Start monitoring the alerts at least 36 hours before the hurricane is to make landfall and stay informed regarding evacuation orders. You may want to investigate having a safe room built that meets FEMA guidelines will withstand strong winds and is high enough to avoid a storm surge.

The best source for hurricane information for the season is your local area's emergency management office and emergency alert center. They will issue updates on what needs to be done if a hurricane is heading in your direction.

If sheltering in place, prepare for high winds and floods. Stay on the lowest floor that will not flood and go to an interior wall away from windows. **Do not forget your pets if you are sheltering in place.**

DO NOT SEEK SHELTER IN AN ATTIC AND IF TOLD TO EVACUATE, DO IT!

Landslides and Mudflows

Landslides and mudflows occur throughout the U.S. and its territories, resulting from earthquakes, storms, volcanic eruptions, and fires. They may also be caused by development or modifications to the land. The wildfires in Santa Barbara destroyed plant life that had secured the soil from erosion, resulting in huge landslides and mudflows from rain that soon followed. It is not necessarily the amount of rain as it is the rate at which the rain falls that triggers landslides and mudflow. The potential for landslides and mudslides can last for years after a fire. Understand your potential risk by getting a proper inspection. Once the risk has been evaluated, experts can make recommendations for mitigation. Planting ground cover is one thing that can be done to help reduce the risk and build retaining walls and other diversion systems for water and debris. Knowing the warning signs for potential problems is important and staying tuned to authorities' alerts.

Extreme Winter Storms

The intensity of extreme winter storms has increased in recent years. If you live in an area with frequent winter storms, you know the need to properly insulate your home and pipes and stay tuned to weather warnings. Before the beginning of the winter storm season, be sure to check your emergency kit and review your plans, including plans, in case your home loses power, or you are confined to your home. The emergency kit in your car should include what you would need if you found yourself stranded in your car. It is also necessary to keep food and water stocked to last at least seven days.

Frostbite is common on fingers, toes, nose, ears, cheeks, and chin. Here are the signs and symptoms:

- Cold prickling feeling of extremities
- Numbness
- Red, white, bluish-white, or grayish-yellow skin
- Hard or waxy-looking skin
- Clumsiness due to joint and muscle stiffness
- Blistering after rewarming

Prolonged exposures cause hypothermia to very cold temperatures, whereby your body begins to lose heat faster than it produces it. Here are the signs and symptoms:

- Blistering after rewarming in severe cases
- Shivering
- Exhaustion
- Confusion
- Fumbling hands
- Memory loss
- Slurred speech
- Drowsiness

Limit the amount of time outdoors and wear layers of clothing when necessary to go out. When shoveling outside, **do not over-exhaust yourself.** Stay off the road as much as possible. Do **NOT** use generators, grills, gas stovetops, or gas ovens to heat the house. Each year, an average of 430 Americans die from carbon monoxide poisoning, more than 20,000 require a visit to an emergency room, and more than 4,000 are hospitalized. These numbers increase over the winter months in part because of the misuse of appliances.

If you have any animals, plan to protect them and have plenty of food and water for them.

Tornados and Summer Storms

According to an article in the Nov 30, 2020, issue of *InsideClimate News,* entitled "Is Climate Change Fueling Tornados?" Penn State University climate researcher Michael Mann said that there is growing evidence that "a warming atmosphere, with more moisture and turbulent energy, favors increasingly large outbreaks of tornadoes, like the outbreak we've witnessed in the last few days." "There is also some evidence that we might be seeing an eastward shift in the regions of tornado genesis—again, consistent with what we are seeing," he added.

Within the same article, Harold Brooks, a senior scientist with the National Severe Storms Laboratory in Norman, Oklahoma, stated that tornadoes are complex, dynamic, short-lived, and small, making them hard to study. But the deadly 2011 outbreak, which included the tornado that tore through Joplin, Missouri, spurred a new wave of studies that help explain how global warming affects tornado activity. In recent years we have seen an increase in the number of tornados, their locations, and their intensity. In 2022 there were 1329 confirmed tornados, in 2023 there were 1378, and as of July 2024 there were already 1259 confirmed.

Brooks also stated that researchers are looking at severe storm development because giant thunderstorms can produce damaging hail and destructive winds even without tornadoes. This is a robust signal that global warming will make the atmosphere more likely to spawn such storms.

To be prepared for a tornado, you need to know where you will go in your home when a tornado warning is issued. If you do not have a safe room that you can escape to, consider having one built that meets FEMA's criteria. It is important to run drills with children to know what to do. Have a plan for your pets, so they are not left outdoors. Pay attention to tornado warning signals and what authorities tell you to do. Make sure you grab your emergency kit to take with you!

Do not attempt to outrun a tornado if you are in a car. Try seeking shelter in a building or underground. If you can safely get much lower than the level of a roadway, get out of the car and lay on the ground in that area with your hands on the back of your head. If there is no significantly lower place, stay in your car with the seatbelt on. Lower your head below the windows and get as low to the bottom of the vehicle as possible. If you have a blanket or jacket, place it over your head and place your hands over your head. You may have heard that it was a good idea to get under an overpass, but that is very dangerous and not recommended as the winds from the tornado can blast debris under the overpass.

Drought

Drought preparedness is all about water conservation. As mentioned previously, in 2022 we experienced the worst drought in 1200 years. Never pour water down the drain if there is something else you can do with it. Almost every part of the U.S. experiences periods of reduced rain. Planning and preparedness during normal rainfall years will equip us for droughts. A few years ago in central California, entire towns ran out of water and had water trucked in. Doing anything you can to conserve water will help to preserve water for dry times.

Things you can do <u>indoors</u> to conserve water:

- If you have dripping faucets, replace washers or the actual faucets themselves if washers do not fix the problem. Just one drop per second uses 2,700 gallons in a year.
- Check for and repair leaks and retrofit faucets, showerheads, and toilets with flow restriction devices.
- Insulate pipes to reduce heat loss and prevent them from breaking in freezing weather.
- Place a one-gallon jug of water into the toilet

tank to reduce water consumption.

- Choose appliances that are water and energy efficient.
- Only use water softener systems when minerals cause damage to pipes.
- Use a compost pile rather than garbage disposal.
- Avoid flushing the toilet unnecessarily, taking long showers or deep baths.
- Do not allow water to run unnecessarily while brushing your teeth, washing your face, or shaving.
- Run the dishwasher only when it is full and use the "smart" water feature, and do not rinse dishes before putting them in the dishwasher.
- Instead of wasting water while you let it get hot or cold, capture water for other uses; otherwise, install an instant water heater or, for cold water, store water in a refrigerator.
- Do laundry only as full loads and use the water conservation feature.

Things you can do <u>outdoors</u> to conserve water:

- Use commercial car washes that recirculate the water.
- Plant native plants or drought-tolerant ground cover, trees, or grasses.
- In drought areas, xeriscape your yard with drought-tolerant plants that require little to no irrigation.

- Group plants together to water multiple plants simultaneously with the same water.
- Use mulch not only to control weeds but also to retain water.
- If you install water features, use circulating water appliances.
- Do NOT purchase water toys that require a constant stream of water.
- Set up a system for saving rainwater. Contact your local water company, as they can give you specific ideas about what will work in your area and how to do it.
- If you have a lawn, use an irrigation system that is water efficient and position sprinklers, so they are watering just the lawn.
- Be vigilant with leaks and broken sprinkler heads. They should be repaired immediately.
- Look at areas around your lawn where you can eliminate some grass and replace it with native shrubs and plants or consider installing the latest generation of artificial turf.

CHAPTER 12

MAN-MADE DISASTERS

Countless types of man-made disasters occur throughout the world. Still, for the sake of brevity, only six will be covered in this book - pandemics, active shooters and mass attacks, household chemical emergencies, cyberattacks, natural gas leaks, and power outages. BePreparedBeReady. org offers courses that detail all man-made disasters and more recommendations on preparing, surviving, and recovering from these disasters.

Epidemics and Pandemic

First, let us discuss the difference between an epidemic and a pandemic. Epidemics are when a disease affects many people in a particular region or country and is out of control and spreading quickly. For example, it was an epidemic when COVID was prevalent in just China. A pandemic is an epidemic that has crossed multiple continents, as we have seen with the worldwide spread of COVID.

Most of us watched daily news reports of toilet paper hoarding, sanitizers, cleaning supplies, food, and water. Few families were prepared! Your emergency kit should already include these items, making a" run" for them unnecessary. Also, you will need a sufficient supply of prescriptions, nonprescription drugs, and other medical supplies. Know how to access your medical records online and have them secured in a fire- and waterproof safe and saved on an external hard drive or in the cloud.

Over the centuries, millions have died due to pandemics, plagues, or other diseases. According to an article in *National Geographic* magazine, published January 31, 2014, and entitled "Two of History's Deadliest Plagues Were Linked, With Implications for Another Outbreak," it is believed that in the sixth century, 30 to 50 million people died in one year, about half of the world's population, from the Justinianic Plague.

Smallpox has been present for hundreds of years and has killed 300 million in the 20th century alone. These large events have been reduced in recent years due to modern medicine, protocols, and technology. What we have learned from COVID is that the virus can continue to mutate and cause outbreaks. Today vaccinations are available each year for different strains. We may never see the end of what started in 2020.

To prevent contagious disease and limit the spread of germs, follow these simple protocols:

- Wash your hands thoroughly for 20 seconds with soap
- Avoid close contact

- Wear a mask - cover your mouth and nose
- Avoid touching your face
- Practice other healthy habits such as getting plenty of sleep, being physically active, managing your stress, drinking plenty of fluids, and eating nutritious food

Active Shooters and Mass Attacks

Unfortunately, this is something we need to discuss; however, it has come to be seen as a sign of the times in our nation. I live in Las Vegas, and on the night of October 1, 2018, we witnessed the horror as 58 people died, gunned down by a lone shooter.

Furthermore, I now know three people who were exposed to active shooters. Never would I have ever thought that I would personally know someone. No one was hurt, but the fact that I know three people who experienced something that could have been so much worse is very scary.

I am very fortunate that I didn't know anyone who was injured or killed in the shooting in Las Vegas; however, I know several people who knew someone who was. My stepson and his wife were supposed to go to the concert and at the last minute decided not to. That event had a huge effect on everyone that calls Vegas home. There was certainly fear and enormous grief. There was also a massive outpouring of support and love for those at the concert who were impacted directly by this mass murderer.

An active shooter is an individual actively engaged in killing or attempting to kill people in a populated area. Mass attacks are defined as the murder of 4 or more persons in a single event. These incidents have underscored the importance of a coordinated response by law enforcement and other emergency services.

What can we do to protect ourselves? First, if you *see* something suspicious, *say* something to the authorities. When entering a building, identify the exits and make yourself aware of possible hiding places.

Many communities offer courses for active shooter training. If confronted with a shooter, *RUN* (they may miss a vital organ or miss you altogether) and try to warn others. If you cannot get away, find a place to hide, such as another room where you should lock and block the doors, turn out the lights and close the blinds. *Do not* hide in groups or spread out along walls—mute your cell phones, including the sound from vibration.

Communicate with the police silently through text messaging. Stay where you are until the police let you know it is okay to come out.

The last resort is to fight! Commit to your actions and act aggressively using whatever weapon is at hand: a chair, fire extinguisher, scissors, or books.

Whether you are directly involved in a shooting situation or are in a community where there has been an incident, consider seeking professional help to deal with the emotional trauma. After the shooting in Las Vegas, services were made available to people living here for many months after the shooting.

Household Chemical Emergencies

Although the risk of a household chemical emergency is minimal, knowing how to handle hazardous household products can reduce the risk of injury. It is important to store household chemicals in places where children cannot reach them.

Products such as aerosol cans of furniture polish, hair spray, deodorant, and bathroom cleaners are considered hazardous materials. Other items include cleaning products, nail polish and polish remover, pesticides, automotive products, kerosene, lighter fluid, and painting supplies.

Always keep products in original containers and never remove the labels unless you need to change the container because the original is corroded. Never mix household chemicals with other products as incompatibility could cause them to ignite, explode or create toxic fumes. If there is a spill, clean it up immediately, put rags in plastic containers and dispose of them in the trash. If a sizable accident occurs, get everyone out of the house immediately!

Symptoms of poisoning include difficulty breathing and irritation of the eyes, skin, or throat. They also include changes in skin color, headache, blurred vision, dizziness, clumsiness or lack of coordination, cramps, and/or diarrhea.

Add the National Capital Poison Control as a contact on your cell phone: 800-222-1222 - and if someone is experiencing any of these conditions, call their number and follow their instructions implicitly. Discard all clothing that may have been contaminated as many chemicals do not wash out thoroughly.

Cyberattacks

A cyberattack is any attempt to gain illegal access to a computer or computer system to cause damage or harm. Hackers, attackers, or intruders use malicious code and attack vulnerable areas. This has led to the creation of cybersecurity, which is the art of protecting networks, devices, and data from these unauthorized accesses. Cybersecurity is important to ensure confidentiality, integrity, and availability of information. What are the risks?

How do you minimize the risk? Keep software up to date, use strong passwords and change them often, use multi-factor authentication, and incorporate firewalls. Be aware of suspicious activity, use secure internet connections, and create backup files.

If an attack happens, take all devices offline, change passwords immediately, and scan and clean the device (you may want to use a professional). Contact banks, credit card companies, and other financial accounts. Additionally, contact credit bureaus and disallow any credit approvals. You should also reach out to the police and Federal Trade Commission, file a report with the Inspector General, and file a complaint with the FBI Internet Crime Center. For online crime, report it to the local Secret Service Electronic Crimes Task Force or Internet Crime Complaint Center.

Natural Gas Incidents

In the U. S., the primary gas sources are natural and propane gas. Natural gas explosions happen when there is a leak that ignites. Over the years, many have been killed or injured due to gas explosions. In 2019, 659 incidents killed 13 and injured 37 people.

To prevent dangerous incidents with natural gas, install a natural gas detector and regularly test the detector. Locate gas lines before digging by calling 811 or going to call811.com.

Maintain all gas appliances and have them checked regularly. Teach everyone in your household how to shut off the main gas valve. If it becomes necessary to turn the gas off, **DO NOT** attempt to turn it back on. Call a professional to turn the gas back on.

If you smell gas, **get out immediately.** *Do not* use a cell phone, turn on a light or anything electrical, and *do not* light a flame. A fire extinguisher should be on hand.

Power Outages

Power outages are on the rise. According to the Department of Energy, the cost to businesses is approximately $150 billion per year. The amount of time that a power outage lasts is now a little over 8 hours. This is mainly caused by the major events that are happening. So, what is being done?

On October 18, 2023, the Department of Energy (DOE) announced up to $3.5 billion for 58 projects across 44 states to strengthen electric grid resilience and reliability. These projects aim to improve climate resilience, create good-paying union jobs, and enhance the overall grid infrastructure.

The GRIP program will leverage more than $8 billion in federal and private investments to address critical grid needs.

To prepare for a power outage, whether a home or a business; take inventory of items that rely on electricity. If there are medical devices, how much power do they require? Determine what is needed for batteries, chargers, and surge protectors. All of this will help to decide the total power that will be needed when the power goes out.

There is a new world of solar-based generators that can produce large amounts of power and are small in design.

Consumer Reports has a comprehensive guide on generators that will help determine what generator will suit the needs of a home or business.

https://www.consumerreports.org/home-garden/generators/buying-guide/

Reducing Energy Use

Whether it is a big appliance or a small charger, if it is unplugged it is not using power.

1. Even though it is impossible to unplug refrigerators, stoves, and other kitchen appliances, think about other small appliances that can be unplugged when you are not using them.
2. Even when all the lights are off, some devices still have lights that glow. Some use super-efficient LEDs, but some power suckers can be turned off.
3. Computers are different. When they go into sleep mode it may be better than turning it off

completely due to the amount of power it takes to turn it back on.

4. If you are going to be gone for some time, turn off everything that is not necessary. Using power strips can make it easy to organize which devices can be turned off until needed.

5. Unless it is a desktop with an old tube monitor, screensavers are unnecessary, and they keep your computer using serious power each time you walk away.

6. An additional benefit of powering off devices is that unless they are designed to stay on at all times, they will last longer by being turned off.

"Saving energy TODAY will make TOMORROW bright"

Swami Vivekananda

CHAPTER 13

OTHER FINANCIAL CRISES

This book is about protecting you, your family, and your business. We have talked about the impact financially of natural and man-made disasters. Then there are crises of other types. Things like a car accident, an illness, the loss of a job or a business, divorce, death, or the inability to make a mortgage payment all play an important role when we are looking at financial and estate planning. Our financial well-being will be greatly impacted in any one of these scenarios.

When we look at our plans and emergency kits, we need to think about what happens when there is a financial loss and how that will affect our lives, jobs, and businesses. When thinking about preparedness, think about what would need to be done if one of these things happened. Create a plan and seek the advice of an attorney, financial advisor, or real estate professional when considering what plans need to be made.

Estate planning is just like a business plan or a resume. They are not something that you can "set it and forget it." That is why just like your emergency kits you need to review and update every year to make sure you have the latest information. Disasters and crises go hand in hand with financial and estate planning.

These are some of the areas to be looked at:

- Illness
- Incapacity (including dementia/ Alzheimer's)
- Death
- Automobile accidents
- Identity theft
- Fraud
- Job Loss
- Care of a loved one
- Emotional trauma
- Foreclosure

CHAPTER 14

RECOVERY SERVICES

There are many recovery services available depending on the disaster and its impact. However, it would be impractical to list them all here. A brief description and a few websites can easily be found for major ones. These include government agencies, non-profits, and faith-based charities. There are wonderful opportunities to volunteer with some of these amazing organizations.

Federal Emergency Management Agency (FEMA)

The Federal Emergency Management Agency, or FEMA, is one of the U.S. Department of Homeland Security (DHS) agencies. FEMA was created in 1979 through an executive order signed by President Jimmy Carter. The history of FEMA dates to the Congressional Act of 1803. This was the first disaster legislation.

FEMA's mission is "Helping people before, during, and after disasters." They are responsible for coordinating the different roles of different governmental agencies, states and regional responses, and other organizations' responses. Several government agencies and programs fall under the FEMA umbrella or work with FEMA. They oversee the preparation, prevention, mitigation, response, and recovery from natural and man-made disasters. FEMA is called into action during a presidentially declared disaster.

In addition, they have individual programs that assist disaster victims. These include mental health and employment programs. Their main program is called Individual Disaster Assistance Program, which ensures that a home is "safe, secure and sanitary".

To be clear, *FEMA is not an insurance company!* FEMA is not there to make someone whole. They provide a flat dollar for items required to make a home safe, secure, and sanitary. These include structural items like roofing, foundation, walls, sheetrock, insulation, paint, and systems, such as HVAC systems and water in the house.

They will provide a flat dollar amount to ensure each household member has necessities, such as a bed, a chair, and utensils for each household member. Provisions include the need for a TV, but they will not replace your 75" latest model. They provide a flat dollar amount for one TV and radio so that households can stay informed for the sake of safety.

National Flood Insurance Program (NFIP)

This agency, which falls under FEMA, was founded in 1968 to determine the level of flood risk in areas and identify the potential as low-, moderate-, or high-risk.

Communities must agree to mitigate and adopt certain control measures to participate in NFIP.

If a property is in a high-risk area, it must carry flood insurance as previously covered. Low- and moderate-risk areas are not required to obtain flood insurance; however, 25% of these properties will experience flooding. In 2018, 15% of homes had flood insurance. That same year, NFIP showed a deficit of $20.5 million. This has led FEMA to mandate that this program be reviewed overall, including updating floodplain maps.

Community Emergency Response Team (CERT)

The Los Angeles City Fire Department gave birth to this program in 1985. In 1993 it became a national program and a part of FEMA. Since it can take up to 48 hours to get first responders into devastated areas, residents must care for themselves in these situations.

CERT provides hands-on training for people in a community to take care of themselves until help arrives. Each community program is based upon the types of risk the community may face. The training includes light search and rescue, fire safety, team organization, and disaster medical training. The training is free and takes about 17.5 hours to complete. The CERT Program is in all fifty states, 2,700 communities and has over 600,000 volunteers.

The U.S. National Response Team (NRT)

Started in 1978, and as part of the then Bureau of Alcohol, Tobacco and Firearms, the U.S. National Response Team was created in response to a significant increase in arson and explosion incidents. Its purpose is to initiate a quick disaster response.

Since its inception, NRT has responded to over 700 incidents. They can respond anywhere in the U.S. within 24 hours. To respond within 24 hours, 13 Regional Response Teams cover the US states, their territories, and possessions. The teams comprise veteran agents experienced in the blast and fire origin-and-cause, forensic chemists, fire protection engineers, explosive enforcement officers, detection canines, and legal, intelligence, and audit support.

National Domestic Preparedness Consortium (NDPC)

Established in 1998, the National Domestic Preparedness Consortium is a FEMA training partner providing high-quality emergency responders training. They conduct training in all 50 states and territories and have trained more than 60,000 state, local, and tribal emergency responders and employees. The training has benefited more than 1.9 million people.

Centers for Disease Control and Prevention (CDC)

Under the U.S. Department of Health and Human Services (HHS), the Centers for Disease Control and Prevention (CDC) is another government agency that plays a key role in disasters and other health risks. In 1946, Dr. Joseph Mountin founded the then Communicable Disease Center. At the time, Dr. Mountin was considered a visionary public health leader and advocated for public health issues. He paid Emory University a token of $10 for the land in Atlanta that the CDC still sits on today.

The CDC's original function was to prevent malaria from spreading across our country. Its main goal is to protect public health and safety by controlling and preventing disease, injury, and disability, both in the U.S. and abroad. In addition to dealing with the prevention of disease and establishing protocols during an outbreak, such as COVID, the CDC's work is vital when it comes to school health, tobacco use, nutrition, obesity, heart disease, stroke, diabetes, cancer prevention, and control, and many other societal health issues.

Non-profits and Other Organizations

Many organizations do amazing humanitarian work when it comes to disasters. Many were started by one or two people that saw a need. If any of these organizations tug at your heart, reach out and join; they would love to have you.

American Red Cross

Founded by Clara Barton in 1881, the American Red Cross' mission statement is, "The Red Cross, born of a desire to bring assistance without discrimination to the wounded on the battlefield, endeavors—in its international and national capacity—to prevent and alleviate human suffering wherever it may be found." Its purpose is to protect life, health, and ensure respect for human beings. In 2019, 306,000 volunteers responded to 60,047 disasters and incidents and provided 529,430 services.

SBP

The SBP (formerly known as the St. Bernard Project) was founded in 2006 by Zack Rosenburg and Liz McCartney as they volunteered at St. Bernard Parish after Hurricane Katrina. They saw the commitment of the people in the community to rebuild but also noticed the painful slowness of the traditional rebuilding processes. They decided to launch an organization to "Shrink Time".

SBP's mission is to rebuild homes quickly, share rebuilding innovations with other rebuilding organizations to improve the process nationally, help communities be better prepared, provide advice to policymakers immediately after a disaster to empower them to recover more quickly, and advocate for reforms in disaster strategies.

SBP is supported and greatly enhanced by AmeriCorp members and boasts 30,000 volunteers. They are supported by donations, volunteers, and corporate partners.

Americares

In 1975, a U.S. jet carrying 243 Vietnamese orphans bound for the United States crashed in the jungle outside of Saigon. One-third of the children were killed, and others were critically injured. The Pentagon said it would take ten days for resources to get to these children. Robert Macauley, a paper broker in Connecticut, heard about the accident and chartered a plane that, 24 hours later, brought the remaining children   to California.

That was the beginning of Americares. It is now the world's leading transporter of medicine and medical supplies. It operates in over 90 countries and all 50 U.S. states. It provides over $500 million of innovative health programs and medical aid each year. "The only thing that's going to save the world is love. Pure and simple. Just love," said Bob Macauley.

Team Rubicon

The Haiti earthquake in 2010 put two U.S. Marine veterans, Jake Wood and William McNulty, into action. They gathered supplies, a small group of volunteers (veterans, medical professionals, and first responders), and went to Haiti. They called themselves Team Rubicon (from the phrase "crossing the Rubicon," which is an idiom meaning passing a point of no return) because they knew there was no turning back from the Dominican Republic into Haiti.

This group helped many who other organizations overlooked. This organization has formed 275 response teams with over   80,000 volunteers. They have served thousands of survivors using their military, medical and leadership skills. They are now a global organization with five separate networks in other countries. They provide effective humanitarian aid in the wake of disasters while "serving veterans by serving others."

All Hands and Hearts

Originally two separate non-profits, All Hands Volunteers (founded by David Campbell in 2005) and Happy Hearts Fund (founded by Petra Nemcova in 2005), they came together in late 2017 to form All Hands and Hearts. They enlist volunteers to work directly with community leaders to meet short- and long-term needs within a disaster area. Their method of helping families recover faster is by using their Smart Response strategy. This strengthens both the volunteers and the communities they serve. Over the last 15 years, they have provided disaster relief to more than 1.1 million people worldwide.

Doctors Without Borders

In May of 1968, a group of French doctors committed to helping victims of wars and major disasters. They are known as Médecins Sans Frontières, or internationally in English as Doctors Without Borders. These doctors were horrified when children were seen dying from hunger and war for the first time on television.

Two of these doctors, Max Recamier and Bernard Kouchner, felt it was important for the world to see what was happening in the province of Biafra, which had seceded from Nigeria and was surrounded by the Nigerian army. They traveled to the war zone, where hospitals performed surgery in areas regularly targeted by the Nigerian army. Civilians were also being murdered and starved by the Nigerian army.

Bernard Kouchner stated, "We wanted to ensure sufficient knowledge of this new type of medicine: war surgery, triage medicine, public health, education, et cetera. It's simple, really: go where the patients are. It seems obvious, but it was a revolutionary concept at the time because borders got in the way. It is no coincidence that we called it 'Médecins Sans Frontières.'"

Today, Doctors Without Borders is in 28 countries, employing 30,000 people worldwide, and since 2014 has completed 8.25 million outpatient consultations.

Direct Relief®

After World War II, William Zimdin, a wealthy immigrant from Estonia, sent thousands of foods, clothing, and medical packages to family, friends, and former employees. He soon dedicated himself to helping the oppressed and established the William Zimdin Foundation in 1948. In 1957, it was renamed Direct Relief Foundation. In 1962, it became licensed as a wholesale pharmacy that developed strict guidelines for the proper types and use of any aid shipments sent to devastated areas.

Their name changed a few more times, and, in 2013, they renamed themselves Direct Relief. Their mission is to improve the health and lives of people affected by poverty or emergencies- without regard to politics, religion, or ability to pay, and to serve "disadvantaged populations living in medically under-served communities throughout the world." They are active in all 50 U.S. states and more than 80 countries. The qualifications of health professionals and inventories are closely looked at.

REACT International, Inc

REACT A group of CB radio volunteers started international, Inc. to assist motorists in 1962. REACT expanded to a network of communication professionals dedicated to helping communities in times of disaster. Their support assists local resources to "accelerate relief efforts".

REACT Teams assist police with public events and traffic control, including providing any special equipment required. Extensive programs have been developed for the relationships between the REACT Teams, emergency services, and governments. Training includes FEMA's courses needed for participation in emergency and disaster communications.

ShelterBox

ShelterBox prides itself on thinking" outside the box." They started in Cornwall, England, as a millennium project through the Rotary Club. Today, it has become a global organization consisting of people who believe in shelter as a human right – that "shelter from the chaos of disaster and conflict is vital."

Where there is a disaster, chaos follows. Losing your home is beyond chaos, as it affects everything you need to do to start the recovery process. ShelterBox promotes stability by reaching out to the most vulnerable in war zone areas like Syria and the Lake Chad Basin.

ShelterBox speeds recovery by providing green box kits with tents, tarps, ropes, nails, tools, and other specific items for rebuilding shelter, depending on where the need is located. They also provide blankets, solar lights, mosquito nets, water filters, containers, and cooking pots. They have helped shelter 1.5 million people in 100 countries since 2000.

UNICEF (United Nations Children's Fund)

Established by the United Nations General Assembly in 1946, UNICEF promotes the rights and well-being of every child. They work in 190 countries and territories to care for the needs of children going through crisis, violence, disasters, and poverty. They promote girls' education, immunizations, the fight against HIV/AIDS, and protecting children from abuse and violence.

They uphold the four core principles of the United Nations Convention on the Child's Rights, including non-discrimination, devotion to the child's best interests, the right to life, survival, development, and respect of the child's views.

NOVA (National Organization for Victims Assistance)

Founded in 1975, NOVA is a recognized leader in victim advocacy, education, and public policy initiatives that protect crime victims' rights. Their mission: "Champion dignity and compassion for those harmed by crime and crisis." Their work includes advocating for victims by connecting them to resources and training advocates and crisis responders. They provide support across the country with over 600 NOVA-trained Crisis Responders delivering education and emotional first aid.

Financial nonprofits

There are several nonprofit organizations out there that can help with financial decisions and concerns.

Need Help Paying Bills

This is a resource for struggling families or single people. They help find nonprofits and other resources that will help with paying bills, job placement, clothing, work items, computers, and other items.

US Government/State Legal-Aid

These agencies provide help with family law including assistance with divorce, domestic abuse cases, child support, custodial disputes, and adult guardianship.

They also assist with civil law including property damage, personal injury, and breaches of contract.

Community Foundations

A community foundation typically supports local charities in a specific geographic area. A community foundation is a public charity that focuses on supporting a geographical area, primarily by facilitating and pooling donations used to address community needs and support local nonprofits.

Charitable Gifting of Real Estate

Real estate is one of the most financially beneficial types of gifts for donors. There are special tax benefits when a property is donated. The tax deduction is based on the fair market value of the home at the time of the sale. This program provides additional benefits over and above the capital gains savings.

Foundation for Financial Planning

The nonprofit's sole purpose is to provide expanded access to pro bono financial planning for people in crisis or need. It is supported by volunteer financial planners to underserved populations, providing them with free, quality advice to improve their finances and their lives.

Faith-Based Organizations

There are hundreds of faith-based organizations that reach out to help victims in need. This list is a sample of a few of them.

The Salvation Army

William Booth, a London minister, took his message to the streets where he ministered to the homeless, the poor, the hungry, and the destitute. The basic services set back in 1878 are still a part of The Salvation Army's mission today. New services have been added to address today's needs in disaster relief. Today, The Salvation Army is in

125 countries.

Volunteers of America

To provide affordable housing and other assistance to low-income people, Volunteers of America was formed in 1896. Thirty-two affiliates have served 1.5 million people each year. They work with older adults, veterans, families, the homeless, people with disabilities, those addicted to drugs, and incarcerated. In 2017, VOA owned 19,000 affordable housing units that helped 25,000 people each year.

Samaritan's Purse

Founded in 1970 by Bob Pierce after visiting suffering children on the Korean island of Koje-do, Samaritan's Purse is a non-denominational Christian organization that helps victims of disasters, wars, poverty, and famine. His mission was "to meet emergency needs in crisis areas through existing evangelical mission agencies and national churches." They provide spiritual and physical help, including women's programs, agricultural help, education, clean water, sanitation, and construction.

NECHAMA Jewish Response to Disaster

NECHAMA, which is "rooted in the Jewish value of Tikkun Olam, 'repairing the world,' engages volunteers in disaster recovery work." Volunteers assist disaster survivors with cleanup, debris removal, sanitizing homes, and repairing homes with sheetrock, insulation, paint, flooring, and more.

Children's Disaster Services

Children's Disaster Services has been helping children since 1980 by setting up childcare centers inside shelters and disaster assistance centers. Their volunteers are professionally trained to work with traumatized children. They go through a rigorous screening process and provide a safe, calm space for the children to heal. Volunteers provide a "Kit of Comfort," filled with special toys that stimulate imagination and encourage children to express their feelings.

Friends Disaster Service

Founded in 1974 after a tornado destroyed Xenia, Ohio, Friends Disaster Service provides volunteers for labor who bring their tools and expertise. They affect each "community and the world: one person, one family, one project at a time." They provide relief for all survivors but will seek out older adults, people with disabilities, low-income families, and the uninsured. They work with other first responders and focus on rebuilding.

Catholic Charities USA®

The mission of Catholic Charities USA is "to provide service to people in need, to advocate for justice in social structures, and to call the entire church and other people of goodwill to do the same." In 1910, four hundred people founded Catholic Charities USA "to bring about a sense of solidarity" among church members that work on different charitable ministries, and "to be an attorney for the poor". In 1990, the task of taking on disasters was added to their response efforts. The volunteers are in communities to provide direct relief when disaster strikes and will be in the community for as long as needed.

If the mission of any of these organizations draws you to them, please reach out to them directly or any others whom you want help when disasters or crises happen.

CHAPTER 15

SUSTAINABILITY

Sustainable living means "Meeting the needs of the present without compromising the ability of future generations to meet their own needs." That means the need to reduce greenhouse gases. The primary greenhouse gases that affect climate change include carbon dioxide, methane, and nitrous oxide, primarily from the burning of fossil fuels. The movement is now toward sustainable electrical energy and reducing coal, natural gas, and petroleum.

In their 2022 Sustainability Summit, the National Association of REALTORS talked about where we are on climate change. Most scientists agree that we need to act now to make changes before it is too late. The ultimate goal is to get greenhouse gases under control and reverse the effects of climate change.

The unfortunate truth is that scientists have been saying the increase in earth's temperature by 2030 needed to be no more than 1.5°c. That level was exceeded in 2023. As of November 2023, the Intergovernmental Panel on Climate Change (IPCC) estimated that the world has a 50% chance of committing to a 1.5°c rise in global warming by the mid-2030s. Scientists are worried that soon the world will have emitted enough greenhouse gases to keep temperatures at this level for far longer. Data suggests that this threshold could be breached as early as 2029.

Scientists say that increasing levels of carbon dioxide and other gases in the atmosphere raise temperatures because they trap in the earth's radiation, creating a greenhouse effect.

A new World Meteorological Organization (WMO) update predicts the development of a La Nina which means cooler conditions in the tropical Pacific near-term but the higher global temperatures in the next five years reflect the continued warming from greenhouse gases.

Arctic warming over the next 5 winters is predicted to be more than 3 times as large as the globe on average.

There are still pathways to avoid irreversible weather patterns, but the window is closing. Nations need to act now. The IPCC offered hope stating that "readily available, and in some cases, highly cost-effective actions than can be undertaken now to reduce GHG emissions, scale up carbon removal and build resilience. The IPCC did affirm that we can still secure a safe, livable future but we need to act now. Action not taken with rising global temperatures also heightens the probability of reaching dangerous tipping points in the climate system that once crossed, can trigger self-amplifying increases in global warming.

UN Secretary-General Antonio Guterres emphasized the urgency of climate action: "This report is a clarion call to massively fast-track climate efforts by every country and every sector and on every timeframe. Our world needs climate action on all fronts: everything, everywhere, all at once."

Researchers from Germany's Potsdam Institute for Climate Research stated, "Climate change will cause massive economic damage within the next 25 years in almost all the countries around the world."

So, what can we do to do our part in becoming sustainable? First, we can listen to our children when they talk about the world, they want to live in. Kids are becoming activists and through their purchasing power are telling businesses everywhere that we want to know what actions they are taking. In addition, Millennials, Gen Z, and Gen Alpha are taking legal action to get their voices heard. These generations represent almost 50 percent of the US population.

Whether purchasing a product or service or investing in a company's stock, they are looking at 2 separate rankings a company needs to be concerned about. The CSR and ESG ratings will be part of their decision of whether they want to do business with a company or not.

What is CSR?

The CSR (Corporate Social Responsibility) rating looks at how a company operates in ways to enhance society and the environment rather than contributing negatively to it.

They look at 4 areas of responsibility:

1. Environmental
2. Ethical
3. Philanthropic
4. Financial

ESG (Environmental, Social, and Governance) is the framework that evaluates a company's policies, culture, and financial factors in investment decision-making.

According to Darren Walker, President of the Ford Foundation; "It's not just 5 percent of your money you give away that matters. What you do with the other 95 percent is almost more important".

Global ESG assets under management hit $30 trillion in 2022 and are on track to surpass $40 trillion by 2030. Investors increasingly believe companies that perform well on ESG are less risky, better positioned for the long term, and better prepared for uncertainty.

What is ESG?

Environmental. Examples include focusing on climate change and carbon emissions, waste management, energy, water, and land usage.

Social. Examples include relationships between the company and its employees, suppliers, customers, community; diversity issues; and responsible marketing.

Governance. Examples include a company's leadership or board structure, executive compensation, and shareholder rights.

If you are doing business with a company, find out their CSR and ESG ratings; as a consumer or business owner, you can encourage companies to increase their rating. In addition to reviewing a company's ESG rating, what can we do as consumers to reduce our carbon footprint? There are companies out there that will determine your carbon footprint.

Small Businesses Benefit from Practicing CSR and ESG

You may be thinking that the ratings are only for big businesses. In fact, it is important. Keep in mind, almost 50% of your customers or clients are Millennials, GenZs' or Gen Alphas'. Practicing CSR and ESG can grow and expand your business. Here are 5 things you can do:

1. Start small, choose a cause that is something your customers and employees care about. Choose a cause that is in alignment with your product or services.
2. Implement business practices that create environmental impact. Things like recycling and using sustainable suppliers for products and services you use.
3. Partnering with other community-based organizations will create volunteer opportunities for employees, suppliers, and customers.
4. Involve employees in deciding what social causes to engage in. That creates loyalty, enthusiasm, and excitement that will be seen in employee productivity.
5. Create a marketing campaign around the cause that promotes your brand.

According to an America Charities Survey, creating a well-designed corporate social program will increase revenue, employee productivity, and engagement, and decrease turnover.

- Increases revenue by as much as 20$
- Increases employee productivity by 13%
- Reduces employee turnover by 50%
- Increases employee engagement up to 7.5%

The Nature Conservancy will provide you with a way to assess your carbon footprint. https://www.nature.org/en-us/get-involved/how-to-help/carbon-footprint-calculator/

Here are some things you can do to make a difference.

1. In this chapter, we cover all of the cash rebates and tax credits made available through the Inflation Reduction Act to create a high-performance home.
2. Other ways to reduce the amount of energy you use. Unplug any items that are not being used. Raise the thermostat in the summer to reduce air conditioning. If you live in a place where you can use a swamp cooler, switch to that as they use a lot less electricity. Use energy-efficient appliances and new efficient light bulbs. Use smart power strips. Install energy-efficient windows and solar screens. Weatherize your home or business.
3. Use renewable energy when possible. Add solar panels to your home or business. Switch to an electric vehicle.
4. Recycle or reuse products wherever possible. Find ways to repurpose items. When recycling, make sure you follow the instructions on correctly putting things in the recycle bin. Things like food containers should be rinsed out before being placed in recycling.

5. Use reusable items whenever possible. Especially try to avoid plastic bottles and other containers as they tend to end up in landfills and can cause harm to the environment and wildlife. Have your reusable straw rather than using plastic straws. When looking for products, look to see if they are eco-friendly, can recyclable, etc.
6. Go paperless as much as you possibly can, and the paper you do accumulate is put in the recycling.
7. Plant a garden. First, growing your fruits and vegetables will ensure you eat food that has not been treated with pesticides. Also, you are eating local and not eating food from Mexico or China. This dramatically reduces the cost of fuel to transport these items to your grocery store.
8. Eat less meat. If you eat meat, use sustainably raised meat and certifiable pasture-raised. Livestock is one of the most significant contributors to greenhouse gases. Have a meatless Monday, which is a worldwide campaign, and you will reduce your meat consumption by about 15%, which means you are reducing the effects of meat consumption by the same amount.
9. Reduce the number of errands you make by planning your trip ahead of time. You can save money on gas and reduce the amount of gas you are using.
10. Conserve water. Look at native plants and zero-scape for your yard. Have a pool or hot tub and have them covered with solar covers. Using drip

systems will reduce the amount of water used outdoors, and if you have a water feature make sure they are recirculating. Indoors use a shower timer to limit shower times. Install low-flow toilets and water-saving faucets. If you do not want to purchase a new toilet, add bricks to the tank to reduce the water used with each flush.

11. Use the dishwasher rather than handwashing dishes and use compost or other scraps rather than garbage disposal.

12. For clothes, wait until you have a full load, wash using cold water versus warm or hot, and use the eco setting.

13. Donate what you don't want and think twice about bringing it into your home—less clutter, and less carbon footprint.

14. Use eco-friendly cleaning products. Rubbing alcohol is a beautiful substitute for cleaning and making your hand sanitizer. It is a disinfectant; it makes counters, stainless steel, and glass shine. Suppose you want that lemon smell with a bit of lemon essential oil or juice. One part 70% rubbing alcohol to 3 parts water will do the trick.

15. Buy fair trade products. If a product has been Fairtrade certified, the company is committed to using sustainable means for production.

16. Speak your voice with your vote

How to Improve Home Performance

Things we can do for home performance that will improve indoor health, conserve energy and water, and provide a better living experience and quality of life:

1. Improved insulation
2. Moisture management
3. Heating and cooling systems (age, efficiency)
4. Whole-house fans or ventilation
5. Appliances (age, efficiency, ENERGY STAR® certification)
6. LED or other energy-efficient lighting
7. Low-volatile organic compound (VOC) paints or Wood
8. Solar & Smart thermostats
9. Natural light

Use sustainable construction to create an eco-friendly home. This is a practice of creating a healthy environment based on 6 ecological principles; conserve, reuse, recycle/renew, protect nature, and create a nontoxic quality environment.

How to Build an Eco-Friendly Home:

1. Consider Eco-Modular Homes
2. Use Recycled Building Materials
3. Build Vertically to Minimize Impact
4. Interior Design with Green in Mind
5. Plan Window Placement Carefully

6. Use Eco-friendly or Recycled Home Products
7. Decorate with Sustainable Furniture
8. Keep Your Utilities Eco-Friendly

How to Create Sustainable Interior Design

When making large purchases for your home look for items made with sustainable materials, that are constructed in a sustainable way using the best ethical production practices.

Sustainable materials can include:

1. Woods
2. Cork
3. Bamboo
4. Paper/Carton
5. Copper
6. Glass
7. Linen
8. Hemp
9. Recycled materials

Here is an example of products that meet these sustainable factors criteria: https://www.foresthomesstore.com/

Inflation Reduction Act, 2022 (IRA)

This bill signed by President Biden in August 2022 represents one of the most significant investments in the American economy, energy security, and climate in

U.S. history. This Act took effect on January 1, 2023. This legislation aims to achieve several key objectives:

Climate and Energy Investments:

The IRA focuses on combating climate change by promoting clean energy and domestic energy production. It creates more than 20 tax incentives for clean energy and manufacturing, encouraging private sector investment and opening access to certain clean energy tax incentives for tax-exempt entities. Additionally, it strengthens supply chains for materials and equipment.

Healthcare and Economic Reforms:

Beyond energy, the IRA lowers prescription drug costs, healthcare expenses, and household energy costs while reducing greenhouse gas emissions. It also enhances economic fairness through corporate tax code reforms and improves customer service at the Internal Revenue Service (IRS). This legislation aims to create good-paying jobs, tackle climate change, and improve services for everyday Americans.

In addition to the IRA benefits, each state has other programs that may be available to consumers. As of this writing, states are still updating those programs, but all the information should be available this year. The good news is that the rebates and tax credits are going to be available until 2032-2033 depending on the benefit.

Here are the different categories of benefits for the Climate and Energy Investment portion of the Act.

High-Efficiency Electric Home Rebate Act (HEEHRA)

The Act allocated $4.5 billion to states for low to moderate-income households with annual income less than 150% of the area's medium income (AMI)

For low-income households with less than 80% of the AMI can receive 100% of the cash rebates up to a maximum of $14,000.

For moderate-income households, with income between 80% and 150% of AMI, they are eligible to receive 50% cash rebates.

Fannie Mae has a website where you can look up what the area medium income is in your area.

https://ami-lookup-tool.fanniemae.com/amilookuptool

Also Pearl Certification provides a site that will let you know what rebates and tax credits your house may qualify for both the IRA and state programs.

https://incentives.greendoor.app

Why is This So Important- The Benefits to the Consumer

1. **Lower Bills Increase Savings-** Over 85% (103 million) will save $37.3 billion a year on energy bills. For households that are using electricity created from coal, oil, or propane would save an average of $496 per year

    a. For low and moderate-income households that save 44%, they would save an average of $377 with many up to $493 each year

2. **Reduces Emissions-** Furnaces, water heaters, dryers, and stoves account for 95% of residential emissions
3. **Electrification Creates Jobs**

    a. 462,430 installation jobs
    b. 80,000 manufacturing jobs
    c. 800,000 indirect and induced jobs

Improves Health with Cleaner Indoor and Outdoor Air

1. Electrifying appliances address the 42% increased risk of children experiencing asthma symptoms associated with gas stoves
2. Indoor pollution disproportionately affects low-income households in smaller homes

3. Outdoor air pollutions of residential buildings account for 15,500 premature deaths.

Examples of High-Efficiency Electric Home Rebate Items

1. Heat pump HVAC systems $8000
2. Heat pump water heaters $1750
3. Heat pump clothes dryers $840
4. Electric stoves and cooktops $840
5. Breaker box $4000
6. Electric wiring $2500
7. Weatherization $1600
8. (Insulation, air sealing, ventilation)

Homeowner Managing Energy Savings (HOMES)

The HOMES allocation is designed to provide rebates to Americans to create more energy-efficient homes but that is where the similarity stops as compared to HEEHRA.

HOMES does not provide point-of-sale rebates on equipment but instead offers rebates based on home performance.

There are 2 types of rebates:

Modeled-performance rebates

1. Low and moderate-income homes that achieve at least 20% but less than 35% are eligible for $4000 or 80% of the project cost
2. Retrofits that achieve energy system savings of at least 35% are eligible for the lesser of $8000 or 80% of the project cost
3. For high-income homes retrofits that achieve energy system savings of at least 20% but less than 35% are legible for the lesser of $2000 or 80% of the project cost
4. Retrofits that achieve energy system savings of at least 35% are eligible for the lesser of $4000 or 80% of the project cost

Measured-performance rebates

1. For low and moderate-income homes, retrofits that achieve energy system savings of at least 15% are eligible for a payment rate per kilowatt hour saved, or kilowatt-hour equivalent saved*, equal to $4000 for a 20% reduction of energy use for the average home in your state or 80% of the project cost.
2. High-income homes with retrofits that achieve energy system savings of at least 15% are eligible for payment rate per kilowatt hour saved*, or kilowatt-hour equivalent saved, equal to $2000 for a 20% reduction of energy used for the

average home in your state or 50% of the project cost.

* Kilowatt-hour equivalent saved is when alternative systems are being used and refers to the energy consumption equivalent to one kilowatt-hour. It's a way to quantify and compare energy usage across different devices or activities

Clean Energy Tax Credit

Homeowners can qualify for a 30% tax credit on purchases or expenditures up to $3200. To qualify for the tax credits each purchase or expenditure has to be linked to a primary residence.

Some Tax Credit Items

1. Solar electricity generators
2. Solar water heaters*
3. Fuel cells and battery storage with a capacity of at least 3 kilowatt hours
4. Small wind energy generators
5. Geothermal heat pumps that meet the ENERGY STAR* requirements
3. *Water heaters are an average of 14%-18% of a home's energy use

Other Weatherization Installs and Energy-efficient

Improvements

1. Home energy audit
    $150
2. New exterior doors (2 doors maximum)
    $250
3. New Exterior windows/skylights
    $600
4. Insulation
    $1200
5. Upgraded electrical panel
    $600

Clean Vehicle Credit

There are new improved credits in regard to electric vehicles (EV). The biggest change is now the $7500 incentive is available at the point of sale rather than when people file their taxes.

1. Eligibility based upon the income of individuals making up to $150,000/household $300,000
2. People incentivized to purchase North American EVS'
3. North American manufactured battery- $3750
4. Batteries constructed with critical minerals extracted from the US or US free trade agreement countries- $3750
5. Previously owned EV vehicles now have a tax credit for up to $4000 or 30% whichever is

lower than the purchase price with a price cap of $25,000

6. The credit available for EVs' bought through dealers
7. They are geared toward low to moderate-income buyers, with an income cap of $75,000/$150,000 joint filers.

You can get a full picture of the savings available for you today, including rebates and tax credits through the IRA and state programs as they come online through Green Door Rebate and Tax Credit Finder. This app will automatically update so you will always have the most up-to-date picture of your savings.

You can search by different locations, filter by product time and program, and pin for favorites for use later. Green Door is a Pearl Certification. They certify the levels of a home's performance. They have 4 levels of performance:

1. **Pearl Asset**- A home that doesn't reach Pearl Silver can qualify for Pearl Asset Certification. This provides useful information about one or more high-performing features in the home and enables the owner to communicate the value of these features to future buyers.
2. **Pearl Silver**- A home with a building shell or a heating and cooling system that is much higher quality than those found in an average home.

3. **Pearl Gold**- A home that has both a building shell and a heating and cooling system that is much higher quality than those found in an average home.

4. **Pearl Platinum**- A home with energy-efficient systems that are far better than those found in an average home. Pearl Platinum homes typically have high-performance features in all four categories.

THE HIGHER THE PERFORMANCE OF A HOME, THE HIGHER VALUE OF THE HOME!

Go to https://www.greendoor.app/

These rebates and tax credits have different dates and requirements to determine when they expire. But most are available until 2031.

CONCLUSION

Hopefully, you have found this book informative and helpful regarding being more sustainable, prepared, and resilient when disasters and other crises strike. If you begin preparing now, it will make you resilient when something happens and help you remain calm.

Instead of thinking, "I really need to do this," you can say, "YES, I did it!" Do not let "Preparedness Procrastination" settle in!

Become resilient! Take care of your family, friends, business team, associates, and community. Help others become resilient, as well.

In addition to becoming resilient and being prepared, examine your carbon footprint. What can you do to reduce your carbon footprint? Sustainability will take time, but if we want a planet that our children and grandchildren can live on, it is our only answer.

One of my favorite stories is by the ancient poet Rumi. He tells the story of a prince coming of age. The king comes to the young man and tells him it is time to go out into the world and gives him one task to accomplish. The prince is gone for a long time, which worries the king.

The king decides to go in search of his son. When the king finds the prince, he goes on and on about everything he has accomplished. The king asks him if he did the one thing he had told him to do. The prince replies, "No," so the king says, "Then it is as if you have done nothing." For me, the king represents God while the prince is humanity. If we do not go into the world and live our purpose, then it is as if we have done nothing.

My passion and purpose is to help Americans be more sustainable, both physically and financially, and be better prepared for disasters. The vision is to help 30 million people. We can help to create a future for our kids, save lives and billions of dollars. When you download your bonuses, you are taking the first steps. Be the one saying "YES"

"Disasters teach us humanity, give us a chance to pause, reflect, and change course." Coni Meyers

ABOUT THE AUTHORS

 Coni Meyers is a force of nature. Her extensive experience and expertise in crisis management and leadership have made her a renowned figure in the field. Coni is a 6X international bestselling author and speaker. She is dedicated to ensuring that individuals and communities become sustainable and are well-prepared during times of disaster.

Coni has tirelessly worked to educate and support thousands of individuals and businesses in their sustainability and crisis preparedness efforts. Her decades of dedication have left a lasting impact on those she has worked with, equipping them with the knowledge and tools to navigate and manage their efforts effectively. As a FEMA inspector, she has played a crucial role in helping communities rebuild and become more resilient.

Coni's impact on the business world is also notable. Two companies she co-founded, WIN Home Inspections and OnlineEd, she helped transform into national enterprises.

Recognizing the need for effective leadership in all spheres of life, she founded CKM Solutions Group, Crystalline Moments Success Movement, and Kickbutt Leadership. These entities focus on inspiring and empowering individuals to reach their full potential.

Coni's vibrant personality is evident in her work and interactions. Full of energy, passion, and grit, she approaches every endeavor with enthusiasm and determination. Her contagious spirit ignites motivation and fosters a sense of purpose in everyone she encounters.

Through her multifaceted contributions and unwavering dedication. Coni Meyers has emerged as a true visionary and leader in sustainability, crisis management and leadership. Her remarkable achievements and commitment to helping others make her an inspirational figure in the field.

 J. Glen Wagstaff, Esq is a licensed attorney recognized with over 50 international awards. He is the founder and managing partner of the nation's largest estate planning law firm and collaborates with thousands of financial professionals in educating the public on financial literacy, estate planning, and insurance.

Over the last 10 years, Glen has handled planning and consulting matters in almost every continent and has advised leaders of nations, billionaires, and large multinational corporations. He regularly sits on the boards of several non-profit organizations including the CKM Preparedness Foundation as well as his foundation.

He is a philanthropist, serial entrepreneur, speaker, and certified coach. Glen lives in Utah with his wife and five kids.

QR CODE INCLUDES BONUS & INFO

OTHER BOOKS BY THE AUTHORS

Crystalline Moments: Discover Your Opportunities and Create Your Best Self

Leadership in Trying Times: Advice to Lead and Succeed

Conceived to Lead: Dismantling the Glass Ceiling Mindset

ADDITIONAL RESOURCES

Department of Homeland Security (www.dhs.gov)

Operational and Support Components within the Department of Homeland Security

- U.S. Citizenship and Immigration Services (USCIS) (www.uscis.gov)
- U.S. Customs and Border Protection (CBP) (www.cbp.gov)
- Federal Emergency Management Agency (FEMA) (www.fema.gov)
- U.S. Immigration and Customs Enforcement (ICE) (www.ice.gov)
- Transportation Security Administration (TSA) (www.tsa.gov)
- United States Coast Guard (USCG) (during times of peace) (www.uscg.mil)
- Cybersecurity and Infrastructure Security Agency (CISA) (www.cisa.gov)

Other agencies that are involved in some phases of disasters

- Central Intelligence Agency (CIA) (www.cia.gov)
- U.S. Department of Agriculture (USDA) (www.usda.gov)
- U.S. Department of Defense (DOD) (dod.defense.gov)
- U.S. Department of Energy (DOE) (www.energy.gov)
- U.S. Department of Health and Human Services (HHS) (www.hhs.gov)
- U.S. Department of the Interior (DOI) (www.doi.gov)
- Center for Domestic Preparedness (cdp.dhs.gov)
- U.S. Department of State (www.state.gov)
- U.S. Department of Transportation (DOT) (www.transportation.gov)
- U.S. Department of the Treasury (home.treasury.gov)
- U.S. Environmental Protection Agency (EPA), Office of Chemical Safety and Pollution Prevention (OCSPP) (www.epa.gov/aboutepa/about-office-chemical-safety-and-pollution-prevention-ocspp)
- Federal Bureau of Investigation (FBI) (www.fbi.gov)
- U.S. Nuclear Regulatory Commission (NRC) (www.nrc.gov)

Agencies under Federal Emergency Management Agency (FEMA) (www.ready.gov)

- National Flood Insurance Program (www.fema.
  gov/flood-insurance)
- Community Emergency Response Team (www.
  ready.gov/cert)
- National Response Team (www.nrt.org)
- National Domestic Preparedness Consortium
  (www.ndpc.us)

Non-profits and Other Organizations

- American Red Cross (www.redcross.org)
- SBP (sbpusa.org)
- Americares (www.americares.org)
- Team Rubicon® (teamrubiconusa.org)
- All Hands and Hearts (www.allhandsandhearts.
  org)
- Doctors Without Borders (www.
  doctorswithoutborders.org)
- Direct Relief® (www.directrelief.org)
- REACT International, Inc. (reactintl.org)
- ShelterBox (www.shelterboxusa.org)
- UNICEF (www.unicefusa.org)
- NOVA (www.trynova.org)

Faith-Based Organizations

- The Salvation Army (www.salvationarmyusa.
  org/usn)
- Volunteers of America® (www.voa.org)
- Samaritan's Purse® (www.samaritanspurse.org)

- NECHAMA Jewish Response to Disaster (nechama.org)
- Children's Disaster Services (www.brethren.org/cds)
- Friends Disaster Services (www.quakersintheworld.org/quakers-in-action/323/Friends-Disaster-Service)
- Catholic Charities USA® (www.catholiccharitiesusa.org)

Financial Nonprofits

- Financial Experts
- www.IMPowerEDnetwork.com
- Need Help Paying Bills Resource
- https://www.needhelppayingbills.com/html/charities_and_organizations_th.html
- US Government Legal Aid
- https://www.usa.gov/legal-aid
-
- Community foundations - https://cof.org/page/community-foundation-locator
- Charitable Gifting of Real Estate
- www.RAOC.com
- Foundation for Financial Planning https://ffpprobono.org/who-we-are/

Thank You!